CRUNCHING GRAVEL

Growing up in the Thirties
by Robert Peters

Mercury House, Incorporated
San Francisco

8/1988

Published in the United States by
Mercury House
San Francisco, California

Distributed to the trade by
Kampmann & Company, Inc.
New York, New York

Earlier versions of "The Butchering" and "The Sow's Head" appeared in *The Sow's Head and Other Poems* (Wayne State University Press, 1968) and *Gauguin's Chair: Selected Poems 1967–1974* (Crossing Press, 1977). A chapter from "Winter" appeared in *Margin* (London, 1986). "Albert," "Rumors of War," and "Halloween" appeared in *Zyzzyva* (San Francisco, 1988).

Mercury House and colophon are registered trademarks of Mercury House, Incorporated

Manufactured in the United States of America

Library of Congress Cataloging-in-Publication Data

Peters, Robert, 1924–
    Crunching gravel : growing up in the thirties / by Robert Peters.
        p. cm.
    ISBN 0–916515–34–6 : $14.95
    1. Peters, Robert, 1924–   – Biography – Youth.   2. Poets, American – 20th century – Biography – Youth.   3. Wisconsin – Social life and customs.   4. Farm life – Wisconsin.
    I. Title.
PS3566.E756Z463   1988
811'.54 – dc 19
    [B]   87–29495
                                                        CIP

For my children,
Rob, Meredith, Richard, and Jefferson,
and for my sisters,
Nell, Marge, and Jane

Blueberries, blueberries, fish and venison. That's what we lived on. But the air was good, though a bit damp and arthuritical in them long winters. You could never heat the house. Near the stove it was so hot you couldn't sit there; yet when you moved away, your back froze. And the floors was always like ice. Your toes warmed up only when you put 'em in hot water or was in bed with quilts heaped over you. Yes, I'd live no place else.

— Charlie Carlson, farmer, bachelor

I remember Bobbie Peters. Sure. He was a baby when he came to my first-grade class. He was three, was potty-trained, and could read all the first-grade books. He'd taught himself by copying ABCs off those cards that came in shredded wheat packages, dividing the biscuit rows. He filled up any paper he found. To show what he'd done, his mother brought cutup brown paper sacks to show his good printing. We let him enter first grade, although he was only three. I helped him write poems and stories. He could never catch a ball, cried a lot, and hung on me too much. I saw him through eighth grade. He's turned into a writer, I hear. That's nice. I still picture him, aged five, standing in front of my desk, holding out yet another of his little stories about some cute animals, Cubby Bear and his friends.

— Dolly Crocker

Bob was bright, though shy, their being so poor and all. If you lived in the sticks you were lice on a pig's behind. All the roads were covered with gravel—no blacktop then. And your shoes crunched walking on it. You had to live in town with plumbing, running water, and electric light to count for much. I loaned Bob a suit of mine (although he was only fourteen, he was my size, 6'3") so he could represent the school in forensics. I guess I was wrong. He stood on that stage in Marshfield, started off good, saw me in the audience, and forgot his lines.

—*E. V. Kracht, high school principal*

I went there to be a lumberjack. But the big timber companies had cut everything down. You had to go way up to the Porcupines in upper Michigan if you aimed to be part of any frontier. I just settled on forty acres in the sticks, and grubbed along raising pigs, chickens, cows, kids, and taters. Sure I wanted more.

—*Herb Jolly, farmer*

Part One: Winter

Snowscape

The storm had piled up a good foot of snow, obliterating the road leading to town. The wind whipped drifts, piling them against the house so that we had to force the kitchen door open. Mounds and hillocks were covered with ice-glaze. Birch and poplar trees were ice-coated; each twig struck by the dazzling sun shimmered. Trees swooped to the ground, so laden with ice their shapes were forever contorted.

To reach the barn, you had to plant each rubber-booted foot slowly, breaking through the glaze to the buried path. A sift of chickadees swept down to eat the seeds of a clump of goldenrod, scattering almost as soon as they landed. The icy air bit your lungs. Your cheeks tingled. The dog stirred from his house. His face was rime white.

Flaring tamarack, pine, and spruce, showing their undersides of green, were perfect mounds of snow, contained, unsullied. Over their tops, distant Minnow Lake glinted with sun, yet another white expanse in this frozen Eden. White smoke drifted from the tin stovepipe secured with baling wire to the roof. The snow had begun to melt around the pipe. You grabbed the nearest birch sapling and shook it, loving the sounds of the cracking ice shattering from the branches.

Accident, Fear

At 1 A.M. the moonlight was so brilliant you could read by it. The fields were still ice-choked, intensifying the light. Only

that morning the county plow had cleared the road leading
to town. I was eleven and sat on my bed gazing out the
upstairs window at the fields and the glorious night. Dad
was in town seeing a friend, playing music. "Look after
Mom," he had said. "You're in charge." I took the responsibility seriously and slept poorly throughout the early part
of the night.

The combination of highland air, chilled temperatures,
and resonant ice and snow amplified sound. The roof
boards snapped so loudly I was sure a raccoon or a skunk
was up there. The hum of an approaching car built slowly.
Weak, jiggling headlights shone. Suddenly, opposite our
house, the car, a Model A Ford, spun out of control and
flipped over on its top, landing halfway up a large drift.
The wheels kept spinning.

I ran downstairs to the kitchen where my mother was
watching through the window. The door was locked.

"He's coming here," Mom said.

The driver had worked himself free from the wreck and
was weaving up the hill.

"Who is he? Who is he?" I whispered.

"I've never seen him," Mom said, pulling me to a corner.
"He's probably drunk."

"Hey, hey," the man called, pounding on the door. "Anybody home?" Silence. More pounding.

"What if he's hurt?"

"Sh. Sh. If he's drunk, he might kill us."

My dad's guns were in the bedroom, useless since I'd
never fired them. Sweat dampened my neck.

The man was in his twenties, husky. We knew everybody
living in Sundsteen. We didn't know him. He returned to
his car and somehow righted it, maneuvering into the road.
He drove off.

The episode lingered like the taste of zinc. I was too
frightened to open the door. I had failed. The code said to
help anyone in need. I had rationalized, saying I had

spared Mom. What if the man was drunk? We never found
out who he was. Dad said he was glad I hadn't opened the
door. "Nobody's within earshot if you'd needed help. You
did right."

Mother

Dorothy Keck Peters (1906–1980) was born near Grand
Forks, North Dakota. She was the eighth of ten children,
five sons and five daughters. Her mother's family, the
Haverlands, was English and her father's family was German. When she was in her early teens, her father was gored
by a bull. He lingered in great pain and died. His sons kept
the farm running.

My parents' marriage was a mix of love and convenience.
Mom's mother had insisted that she either marry or get a job
in town, for she could no longer live at home. She was taller
than most women, slender, with luxuriant black hair that
began to gray before she was thirty. She was immaculate.
Although she was poorly educated she had completed a year
of high school in Grand Forks — she believed in education. In
1923, when she was sixteen, she met Sam Peters, an itinerant
member of the seasonal threshing crew. He was twenty.

That September they married and drove in a Model T
Ford to Wisconsin, where Sam's brother Geshom ("Pete")
was settled. My mother was soon pregnant, which did little
to still her loneliness, dumped as she was into extreme
isolation three miles from the nearest town, Eagle River.
Her sister-in-law lived nearby, but Kate was strange. This
French Canadian woman was superstitious, had sent an old
man to prison for ostensibly raping her, had an illegitimate
son who shot himself when he was twenty-one, and gave the
illusion of awesome powers. My mother, for self-protection,
saw as little of her as possible.

My father worked in town as a mechanic, which meant that my mother was alone much of the time. The house, built of heavy hewn logs cut by my dad's father, Richard, was utterly primitive. There was an outhouse, and water had to be pumped outside. My mother, hardly more than a girl, worried that a doctor would not be available when she needed him. A month after her seventeenth birthday, I was born. She named me after Robert Louis Stevenson. *A Child's Garden of Verses* was the only book we owned.

Watering the Cows

At 4:30 P.M. the school bus dropped me off. It was already dark. I wrapped my muffler around my face and rushed to the house. The shed windows were already frosted. Icicles four foot long hung beside the door. Wisps of smoke floated from the metal chimney pipes. The roof snapped and cracked under its burden of snow, on this, one of the coldest days of winter.

I hastily changed my wool slacks for overalls. Each lost minute would make watering the cows more difficult. The pump would be frozen, and the cow and her bull calf would be incredibly thirsty — they hadn't had water for twenty-four hours.

I grabbed a hot water kettle and hurried to the pump. The handle resisted at first. I grabbed a half-barrel, freed the bottom of ice by kicking it, and shoved it under the spout. Steaming water spewed forth.

Lady pulled free of her chain, dashed off a few yards into deep snow, wallowed, pulled free, returned to the path and waited for her calf. As she drank, her head was lost in steaming, freezing air. When she was sated, I emptied the tub, and turned it over in case of heavy snow.

Returning to the barn, I forked timothy and clover. As the cattle ate, I shoveled manure through a trap door, cleaning the stalls by lantern light. I secured the animals and returned to the house. In another hour and a half I would milk Lady.

In the living room, I crowded near the potbellied stove. The sides were red-hot. Pitch pine was burning. Pine takes fire the moment a match touches it. I brought the kerosene lamp to the table's edge. Holding my Latin book near the lamp, I read the new declension. I would review it several times before supper and again later while I milked. By bedtime—about 8:30—I'd have it memorized. In the morning I'd brush up on the way to school. There was also algebra, which gave me trouble. Most nights I finished about half the math homework. The ruthless logical relations of parts drove me crazy. I felt stupid, so I took as much math as I could. My report card showed A's in other subjects, while math hovered at C.

After a supper of potatoes and eggs fried in bacon grease, tinned Argentine beef, courtesy of County Welfare, dill pickles made by my mother, canned green beans, and bread and butter, I returned to the barn. I wiped Lady's udder, then began the slow-pressured squeeze. I loved the sound of milk striking metal—like tiny explosions blended with shredding silk. The gray cat sat nearby. When the pail was nearly filled, I stripped the teats; then I checked to be sure that Lady had bedding, and I extinguished the lantern.

The stars were close enough to touch. The horizon shimmered with northern light. No wind. Land and trees suspended in crystal—the advent of an extreme chill. Inside their shed the pigs whiffled. Not a sound came from the henhouse. Later, my dad would start a fire in the gas-tank heater. On such brilliant nights my usual fear of the dark eased—no wolves, bear, or wild men of the woods would sally forth in such cold. The light from the living room window, though feebly cast, was magnified in the subarctic air. It fell over the snow at my feet like daffodils.

The House

Built of logs and axe-hewn beams, our new house sat on a knoll flanked by white birch, Norway pine, and spruce. It looked thrown together as if by a troll—the hip-roofed upper storey, with its tiny cross-paned window facing the gravel road, was askew. The surface plaster was a dismal gray. The northern hip was longer than the southern. And the weathered clapboards were badly chinked with moss and plaster. From the roof emerged a thin blue tin stovepipe, anchored to the roof with baling wire. As if the soot were burning, sparks flew, expiring on the snow.

The lower storey fit snugly into a tree-covered hill complete with a root cellar. An unpainted gray clapboard shed, jerry-built, was affixed to the lower storey, as a kitchen and storage room for mops, pails, and winter clothing. The stoop, which my mother kept brushed clean, was of cheap pine boards painted blue. All around the house, from the eaves, hung long icicles, some as tall as a boy.

Beside the cardboard-insulated door, the snow was stained where we relieved ourselves in cold weather. In spring, the weeds were luxuriant, for we also dumped dishwater there. Nearby, bared to the elements, was a small green pitcher pump, the source of our water. Beneath a wooden platform, layers of straw protected the pump from freezing.

Fronting the house was an area fenced with wire, holding dead bachelor's buttons and withered cornstalks. Beyond, snow-piled, was a three-acre field for potatoes, cabbage, turnips, onions, and strawberries. A shoveled path led down a short incline to the graveled Sundsteen Road. Snow banks were shoulder-high, with excavations hollowed out as ice caves by my sister and me. Our mailbox, with its red metal flag, was across the road, set for easy access by the mailman, Francis Sailer.

We could see the Kula farm. Mrs. Kula labored in the fields and spoke only Polish. She always wore a white babushka. Her husband was a hard-working man of great rages who cursed both sons and horses. The Kulas made little effort to fit American ways; they might just as well have been tilling fields near Kraków.

Doing the Wash

On the night before we washed clothes I filled two galvanized rinse tubs and set them in the unheated outer shed attached to the kitchen. In the morning we would have to remove the layer of ice formed during the night. We ladled hot water from a copper boiler into a primitive hand-crank washing machine. My job was to work the agitator. We started off with all the whites, squeezing them by hand into the first rinse, prepared with blueing, and then a second rinse. Mom and I took turns hanging the clothes outside; it was my chore to shovel snow from beneath the lines. In a few minutes, even if you wore gloves, the dampness from the wash froze your fingers, and you had to go inside to warm them. Soon we were finished, and the clothes on the line were board-stiff. The sheets we dried in the kitchen and living room on rope strung up for the purpose. I loved the fragrance of fresh starch in the antiseptic frigid air. Years later, my mother blamed these conditions for her arthritis.

Movies

The Saturday before Christmas, Dad gave my sister Margie and me a quarter apiece for a matinee. It would be dark when we got out after the double feature. The weather was cold and clear. "Walk fast and you'll stay warm," Dad said. I had never before seen a movie.

We arrived just as the first film began and found our seats in the dark. The credits appeared: *Rose Marie*, starring Jeanette MacDonald and Nelson Eddy. I believed every moment. I knew that Jeanette could position herself on a real Rocky Mountain peak on a moonlit night, warble "Indian Love Call" across the intervening canyons, and be heard by Nelson Eddy, clad in his Canadian Mountie uniform, seated on yet another peak listening and returning the song. MacDonald was an apparition made filmy and mystical via the soft-focus effect of the camera's lens. And how I wished that Eddy were my father leading that cadre of Royal Mounties in immaculate close-order drill through the vastness of those mountains.

The second film was a shocker, an exploitation film on the Ku Klux Klan and the lynchings, torturings, and burnings of southern blacks. I had been only dimly aware of that vicious social history.

I left the theater dazed and took Margie's hand as we walked through the town toward Sundsteen Road. It was already dark, and a soft drift of new snow was falling. I loved the play of the flakes in the arc of dim light around the street lamps.

I nagged Margie to walk faster. I listened intently for strange noises in the underbrush, knowing that no hooded men would jump forth to kidnap us. I imagined a hanged man swaying from a tree silhouetted against the sky, a few feet away in a marsh. Owl hoots were ominous. A deer, startled by us, crashed into the woods. Still holding Margie's hand, I began to run. "Don't, don't," she called. "'Fraidy cat."

In twenty minutes we were home regaling our parents with lurid details about the Klan. I could barely eat supper.

Father

Samuel Peters (1902–1969) was from a German-Irish family, traced by a Mormon cousin back to a Tunis Peters who emigrated to America in the eighteenth century. When Sam was two, his mother died of a ruptured appendix and German measles, and Sam was raised by an older sister in a North Dakota prairie sod house. His dad, Richard, scavenged mines for a living and was gone for days at a time. Five years later, the sister disappeared, and Sam was alone, isolated from neighbors. His only food was sourdough pancakes, which he would bake over a primitive cookstove using wood he himself gathered. All of his life, his breakfasts included these pancakes, made with bacon drippings and topped with sugar.

His formal schooling consisted of two grades in a one-roomed prairie school. Eventually he became a carnival roustabout, worker on threshing crews, and mechanic. Though semiliterate, he believed in education. He taught himself electronics and to play musical instruments by ear—accordian, banjo, mandolin, fiddle, and guitar. He had a special gift for colorful verbal images and was popular in bars and at work.

He built our house and outbuildings, fashioned a saw machine from an old Model T engine, managed our livestock and farm, fished and hunted, and provided us with much physical affection. He grew easily disgruntled with bosses and foremen and often quit jobs. In the 1960s he established his own blacksmith shop. He suffered lower back problems. He was over 6' and always listed to accommodate his back. Despite the poverty, the bad teeth, the coughing, and the wrenched sacrum, he seldom complained. Perhaps since his own mother died when he was a babe, his Dorothy was both wife and mother to him. He often resembled a jolly, big child. In his fifties he contracted stomach cancer: All his life he had downed baking soda and drunk much beer. One morning at the Lincoln town dump, where he was the caretaker, he shot a stray dog, had a heart attack, fell into some flames, and died. He was only sixty.

Lovers' Plunge

"Yes, there's where it went in," Dad said, pointing to the smashed wooden bridge. "Want a closer look?"

He took our hands and we walked to the very spot where Rick Burns had lost control of his Chevy and plunged into the icy water. His high school sweetheart and fiancée, Marjorie Price, was with him. They were still both down there under the broken ice, in who knew how many feet of water. The ice was about two feet thick, normal for late November, even when the current was swift, as it was here. Black water roiled on to the junction with the Wisconsin River, beyond the bridge.

"They slid on a patch of ice," Dad said. "They say Burns wasn't a drinker."

I had seen Marjorie Price a couple of times walking to town. She had lived with her parents just a few houses south of Sundsteen Road. What a harrowing death! Had she grasped Rick Burns to her as they drowned? Were they still locked in a lovers' embrace?

"The sheriff's coming with a tow truck."

"I don't want to stay," I said to Dad. "Take us home."

"Sure," Dad said.

A number of cars were parked now, waiting.

Later, Dad saw the bodies in the car as hoists and winches raised the Chevy. Although there was no chance of reviving them, the deputies pumped their chests.

The Farm Buildings

Walk past the outhouse, a two-seater, with the ubiquitous Sears, Roebuck catalogue handy for wiping, toward two log buildings half buried in snow. One was the chicken coop. On warm days the hens and the single-combed white leghorn rooster ate grain scattered in the snow of a fenced-in yard. The rooster, who crowed incessantly, had trouble standing since all of his toes froze off during forty degree below zero weather. We called him "Crip." He was a pet. He did his business well — most of our eggs produced chicks. The interior of the coop was dark but whitewashed, with nesting boxes. A triple set of roosts fashioned from birch poles accommodated thirty hens. In the very center, buried in the floor, was an old gas-tank heater.

Our cow, Lady, and her yearling occupied the other barn. Lady's stall was nearest the door. Near the top of the wall was a trap door for light and for throwing out manure. By spring, the manure pile, which we stoneboated to the fields, was taller than the barn. The stoneboat was made of planks mounted on wide sled-runners, which was drawn by horses. A mound of hay, cut by my father in neighbors' fields, along the public roads, and in the marshes, stood sheltered by some fir trees.

Near the barn, on a path leading to Minnow Lake, was the pigsty. We kept three pigs, a sow and two of her last litter. Even on the coldest days, they rooted through snow and fussed and quarreled over their swill. Their floorless shelter, which we maintained with straw, was made of saplings, with a tar-paper roof. The pigs were white with large black spots. They crowded together for warmth. Icicles hung from their mouths. Their eyes frosted over.

Half of our forty was arable. The rest was given over to swamps. The frontage on Sundsteen Road adjoined my uncle Pete's property and marshy state lands. Most of our farm was sandy. The rest was in trees. A creek choked with dead logs emptied into Minnow Lake, known for its thick muddy bottom. Leeches swarmed there. When we stocked the lake with bass and crappie fingerlings, the blood-suckers disappeared and the scavenger perch diminished. We tried excavating lake mud with buckets and shovels but soon gave up on ever having a sandy place to swim. There were extensive cranberry marshes. Across the lake, hills led to my uncle's farm. Beyond it lay the impeccable Ewald forty.

Dad bought our farm through the Homeowners' Loan Corporation, established by Franklin D. Roosevelt. The loan, arranged through the local First National Bank, was for $250. All $40-per-month payments were waived until Dad found work as a mechanic and could leave his job, which paid $10 per week.

The Swedes

"What's he doin' settin' there? Waitin' for roses to bloom?" George Jolly first noticed Lars the Swede, half covered with snow, sitting on the front stoop. His hands were stiff along his sides. Leaning back against the front door, he appeared to be sleeping.

Lars and a friend, Carl, lived in the green tar-paper shanty a quarter of a mile from the Jolly farm. It was the last dwelling you passed before entering the forest leading to Columbus Lake. George, his brother Bill, and I were going to the woods to check muskrat traps.

"He's dead," said George, peering into the man's face. "He froze to death." George looked in the front window, then pounded on the door. No response. Carl was not there—or was he inside, frozen too? No smoke came from the roof pipe. Since the men were heavy boozers, we guessed that Lars had come home drunk, had found the door locked, had no keys, and had fallen asleep sitting in the snow, waiting for Carl. The freezing would have been gradual. Lars's lips were a purplish blue. His eyelids were covered with rime, as was his short sandy beard.

"Come on," Bill said. "Let's go tell Dad."

"I'll stay here and watch," George said. "I don't want no animal chewin' on him." He turned to me. "Bob, stay here."

The vigil seemed interminable. Death stained the surrounding air with a lethal dye. Earlier, standing on the bridge looking down at the hole in the ice where the lovers awaited rescue, I had felt something both frigid and sultry, something quasi-mystical. A filament of spun glass connected me to the Swede. The filament drew me toward death. *I would not go! I did not want to go!* Death was a patina of green decay, worms, and fatty exudations from the eyes, ears, and nose. I was ill-prepared for the strange blend of death and life in the Swede's peaceful corpse.

Kitchen

To enter the kitchen, you passed galvanized washtubs, a copper boiler, a clothes wringer, a rick of firewood, mackinaws, fur-lined caps, and mittens on spikes. Opposite were unpainted pine cabinets. We couldn't afford paint. The cupboards had defective knotholes and flangings. Knobs on the doors were empty sewing-thread spools. Each door had a small Guernsey cow clipped from an evaporated milk can. There was also a thermometer, courtesy of Brandner's Grocery where my father charged groceries.

A counter held canisters of flour, sugar, salt, and an old blue roasting pan used for washing dishes. Dishrags hung from hooks. Below there were more cupboards. Near the door were two galvanized water pails. There was a dipper, which the entire family used for drinking. My sister and I took turns filling the pails. On the coldest days, once we had thawed the pump, we filled the wash boiler to be sure we didn't run out before we could reprime the pump.

The Home Comfort kitchen range, of cast iron, had a myriad of uses. It was wood-burning, which meant that my mother needed ingenuity to bake bread. Warming ovens stored fry pans and kettles. Ornamental aluminum strips curved down the sides. A reservoir unit for holding warm water adjoined the firebox. Within easy reach sat a covered wooden crate for holding wood. Each day it was refilled from outside ricks. The oven had neither window nor thermometer. You inserted a hand to see when the oven was hot. On a window ledge nearby were cleaning powders, soap, and a straggly Christmas cactus.

You were struck immediately by the unfinished nature of the living room. My father had never covered the studs, and had instead tacked up old newspapers and flattened boxes for insulation. Culled pine boards, considered too imperfect by the lumber company to sell, protected us from some of the cold. Nail ends securing tar-paper protruded from the roof.

Despite its limitations, the room was cozy. A round oak table with much-chipped and ill-matched chairs sat near the kitchen. White china plates, cups and saucers, glasses, and much-abused flatware, plus an array of condiments. Behind the heater were hooks for drying clothes. A pair of small windows facing the yard were curtained with flannel. Two varnished rocking chairs. A shelf with a radio. We were waiting for Kate Smith to sing "When the Moon Comes Over the Mountain." A sky radiant with northern lights produced the best reception. On other nights, we could hear only by clustering near the speaker. Dad was taking a correspondence course from the De Forest electronic school. Mom studied with him, teaching him to pronounce and understand the words he didn't know. He turned pages by first wetting his finger with his tongue. His hands were large. Car grease was embedded in the skin around his cuticles. He was excited when his papers earned A's.

Root-Cellar Rat

To reach the cellar you raised a door in the center of the living room. A crudely fashioned ladder led down into a black stench of decaying potatoes, onions, and carrots blended with damp seepage from earthen walls. It was advisable to cast a light before you descended. Shelves filled with mason jars were crammed with string beans, peas, carrots, beets, rhubarb, strawberries, wild blueberries, juneberries, raspberries, pickles, and watermelon preserves. There were also jars of chicken, venison, and pork. Potatoes buried in sand had started to sprout, sending out long, anemic, serpentine roots. Onions hung in bags from nails. There was also a crock of sauerkraut and the last of Dad's home brew. My parents did well at gauging the amount of food we'd need. The cellar hole, about seven feet deep, sat well below the frost line.

We heard a rat thumping in the cellar. Finally, our flashlight spied him. Dad knocked a wooden box apart, trimming the boards, narrowing the trap. He tied the trap door with a buckskin string and inserted a chunk of Welfare cheese. When the creature ate, the string would snap the door shut.

On the third morning Dad had just left for work driving the Vilas County Relief truck when Mom and I heard a terrific clatter. We'd caught him! I climbed into the pit and retrieved the box with its enraged prisoner. He was the largest rat I'd ever seen.

Mom removed the stove lid. I positioned the trap over the fire, with the door toward the flames. The rat's frantic movements shook the box. With a heated poker I beat his toes, forcing him into the flames. Screams, the smell of singed fur.

Rooms

From the living room, one ascended two steps to my parents' bedroom. The double bed had a brown metal frame, a cotton mattress, sheets of bleached flour sacks, and two patchwork comforters. Above the bed were a newspaper photo of Jesus cradling a lamb, a photo of my grandmother, and my parents' wedding picture in an oval metal frame with a cluster of metal flowers at the base. In this portrait, my mother wore her hair in bangs, as was the fashion in 1923, and a string of fake pearls. My father wore a dark suit with a white shirt and tie; his hair was cropped at the sides. He was twenty, my mother sixteen.

On the floor was a hooked rug my mother had made. My parents' clothes hung from a birch pole angled across a corner. Like the living room, this room was unfinished. There was an old stool covered with geraniums, now dormant, in metal cans. Near the door was my four-year-old sister Nell's cot. Apple crates held her clothes, dolls, and coloring books.

More rough-plank stairs led to an overhead bedroom. As you ascended you might scrape your skull on the vicious ends of tar-paper nails projecting through the roof. There were crates for books and toys. Our play area was adjacent to a tin stovepipe. Well-worn linoleum protected our knees from wood slivers. Standing erect was possible only in the center of the room. The hip roof saved heat, but also induced claustrophobia. Small paned windows, askew, were in both ends of the room. Thin curtains on string covered the icy glass. No wall was finished, nor were the window frames and sills painted. A double bed occupied the far corner. Here I slept with Everett, five years younger, under a heavy quilt made of colored worsted scraps. Since the quilt was too heavy to wash by hand, it accumulated much boy-soil. The pillows were bleached flour sacks crammed with hen feathers.

On an orange crate beside the bed sat a single-wick glass kerosene lamp on a crocheted doily. In the crate were a book of Lutheran prayers and a much-thumbed King James Bible. I read from the Bible night and morning. I intended to read the entire Bible aloud, including the genealogical names. I loved the Doré illustrations, especially the one of Daniel in the lion's den. In recurring dreams Daniel visited me.

Indians

At 6 A.M. the ice was ablaze in sunshine. Ice-covered birches bent to the ground. Lakes were smothered with freshly fallen snow.

My father and I were driving in the County Welfare truck to the Lac du Flambeau Indian reservation for a truckload of cotton comforters sewn by Flambeau women, as a U.S. government relief project. The reservation was eighty miles from Eagle River. For months the women had met daily at the Community Hall to sew quilts of cotton batting and flowered cloth supplied by the government. Dad would distribute them to needy families.

Some Indians lived on the outskirts of Eagle River and in nearby Clearwater. The largest Indian family had our name, Peters. We were not as impoverished as they, and we shared many of the overt prejudices of whites then against Indians. We were sure we bathed more, drank less alcohol, avoided knife fights, and rarely beat our wives and kids. The girls from the "other" Peters clan were regarded as unteachable and usually left high school pregnant. Indian yards swarmed with dirty kids, straggly hens, and mangy hounds (we even believed that they made stew of their dogs). Junked cars completed the scene. A white man marrying an Indian woman was ostracized as a "squaw man." One white lumberjack, George Petts, married an Indian and lived on the highway to Rhinelander. He joked about his squaw's fertility—she "squirted" forth a "papoose" a year. At last count, there were eight kids. Petts was a notorious poacher. Apprehended, he pleaded poverty, saying that if the county jailed him, they'd have to feed his family. The authorities usually let him go.

Lac du Flambeau was located at a confluence of lakes and rivers, with much virgin timber nearby. The town itself was home to three hundred souls, most of whom lived in bark shanties. Tourists avoided the town, preferring not to be distressed by the obvious and extreme want. The Works Progress Administration, as an employment project, built weather-sealed outhouses—one per family. These were of first-quality lumber, painted in bright colors, and far superior to any of the houses they graced. We joked that the Indians would be far more comfortable in their outhouses than in their shacks and wigwams.

A huge squaw wearing a cheap gingham dress, with a bib apron of a clashing flower pattern, met us. Her graying hair hung full about her chubby face. With a meaty hand she gestured us into the hall where a dozen or so women sat around plank tables working. The odor was a mix of skunk and human sweat.

We loaded the truck. As we worked, Dad joshed with the squaws. He preferred delivering welfare to these people than to needy whites.

By mid-afternoon, back in town, we unloaded the truck. At home, I scrubbed myself, trying to efface the odor. We hung our clothes outside in the icy air, but the smell persisted.

School

The Sundsteen School was a white clapboard single-room affair, without basement, situated on bare land at a juncture of roads. Sundsteen Road veered west here and wound on, meeting Highway 17, which led eventually to Rhinelander, the largest town. The road past the school was little more than a two-mile service road ending near swamps leading to Columbus Lake. Several of the poorest families lived along this road, far from town.

At the front of the schoolroom were the teacher's desk, a blackboard, and a large wood stove enclosed in corrugated tin ineptly stamped with metal flowers and grapes. Twenty movable desks were arrayed before the teacher, the first-graders to the front, the eighth-graders to the rear. On cold days, we pulled chairs as close to the stove as possible. The "library" was a bookcase roughly six feet high and six feet wide holding a scattering of much-abused books and a set of Compton's Encyclopedia. Beside the bookcase sat what we called a "sandbox," a long mahogany-stained pine case standing on what appeared to be piano legs and filled with sand. Here we built relief maps of the area, complete with glass for lakes and twigs for trees. Occasionally, some enterprising student drew an approximation of Wisconsin. In spring the box held quarts of frogs' eggs, which we observed hatching. If the tadpoles did not die, we returned them to the swamps where we had found the eggs.

Igloo

I would do anything for Osmo Makinnen, the school bully, although, since I was nearly three years behind my class in age, I was often the butt of his teasing. Provoking my tears was easy, and when I complained, the others called me "sissy" and "teacher's pet." Miss Crocker could do little but comfort me. She was seldom with us on the playground, particularly in winter, when we donned our wool coats, hats, mufflers, and rubber boots and swirled around the school like insane starlings.

One winter, after the heaviest snowfall of the year had hardened into drifts, Osmo and his cohorts excavated an enormous tunnel in the snow the county plow had pushed back from the road—massive deposits of hard snow covered with an icy crust. The tunnel led to an igloo large enough for three persons.

Osmo began the excavations by explaining his plans for the room, which we would use as a clubroom. He delegated most of the digging but ignored my anxious wish to contribute. I should have known better. Showing his disregard, even contempt, for me, he passed the shovel over my head to my cousin Grace, who stuck out her tongue. I hung about, pathetically trying to catch his eye.

For the next week, until the digging was over, I stayed by myself, made snowmen, and followed fox-and-geese patterns, pretending that others were also playing the game.

I was surprised when Osmo said he wanted me to be the first to enter. He insisted on an early start, to leave time for the others to visit before classes started again. I didn't even bother to eat my lunch.

He first removed the end of an old barrel blocking the entrance. "You'll have to crawl all the way back," he said. "I'll be right behind."

The passageway was barely wide enough for my shoulders. I negotiated a turn by squirming along on my belly. Osmo had warned me not to kick the tunnel sides. The roof of the igloo was built of snow blocks, each dovetailed and rounding to form a domed roof. Sunlight shimmered through the roof, a lovely iridescent green.

Osmo asked my opinion of the place. I said it was great. I imagined Eskimos safe inside from an arctic blizzard. Osmo took a handful of wood shavings and some twigs from his pocket, scooped out a spot in the floor, and struck a large wooden match to start a fire. He unwrapped a small packet of waxed paper, revealing two small strips of venison. "Your lunch," he said, holding the meat over the flames. "Big hunter come from hunt." The meat looked juicy. He took the first scrap for himself, then handed me the second.

He ordered me to stay while he went for the others. I heard voices at the far end of the tunnel, then laughter. The igloo shook. I started toward the passageway and was horrified to find it blocked. They were crushing the whole thing in on me!

Fighting panic, I returned to the igloo, finding it hard to breathe. I was too short to reach the domed roof. Would death be like this—ice-breath seeping through my skull?

I thought I heard Osmo's voice. I was wrong. They had returned to classes, leaving me there. I would not cry! Slowly, I began to dig with my hands where the entrance had been. I shoved snow in behind me. I cleared a few feet but realized I was getting nowhere. The compacted snow was too deep.

I found a block of frozen mud, scraped up by the snowplow, which I flung against the roof. It broke through! The tumbling snow formed a mound, which made it easier to reach the roof blocks, to push them by hand. I was free!

Our Food

We used bacon grease for frying eggs, stirred it into bread batter and biscuits, and mixed it with Welfare peanut butter to make the spread go further. Peanut butter usually

came wrapped in butcher paper. We filled lard pails half
full, set them on the stove reservoir to warm, and then
mixed in bacon drippings. The result was delicious — salty,
smoky, and loaded with calories and cholesterol.

We churned our own butter from Lady's cream in a
gallon-sized glass jar with screw-on top and wooden pad-
dles and handle. It took half an hour of vigorous churning.
We loved the buttermilk. When Lady's supply of cream
didn't suffice, Dad bought oleomargarine, which in those
days could not be colored since it would pass as butter,
something prevented by the powerful Wisconsin dairy
lobby. We dumped the pale oleo into a mixing bowl,
opened up a bead of orange dye, and proceeded to color
the oleo to resemble butter. It seemed more palatable that
way. Colorless oleo resembled lard, something only truly
destitute people ate on bread.

Twice a week we baked bread. The flour, from government surplus, came in fifty-pound cloth bags. None of
these were wasted — all were bleached and sewn by my
mother into dresses, shirts, sheets, towels, and handkerchiefs. We begged for bits of yeast cake to eat. Once the
dough was kneaded, we turned the loaves out into heavily
greased tins, black from use, and stuck them in the warming oven to rise. We stocked wood — pitch pine if we had it —
until the stove was hot. Mom fried pieces of bread dough in
deep grease. These "fritters" were delicious smothered in
peanut butter and sugar!

We seldom had meatless days. The staple, which we soon
tired of, was corned beef from Argentina. "Not to be Sold"
was stamped in black letters on the gray tins, followed by
"U. S. Department of Agriculture." I liked the meat best
either straight from the can, cold, in huge forkfuls, or
warmed with peas. We had variety, too: In the fall, at
Thanksgiving, we had venison, and later a butchered pig
or a yearling calf. Chicken, a special treat, was reserved for
holidays and an occasional Sunday. In late summer, when
we culled the new flock, we frequently had chicken.

Butcherings occurred shortly after the first snows. The semiarctic cold would preserve the meat, cut into roasts and chops, wrapped in butcher paper, and hidden in snow on the roof of the house, secure from thieving dogs, skunks, and coyotes. Most meat, except for the occasional roast, we fried or braised, usually with sliced and fried potatoes. We would never eat sausage made from animal blood, in the German fashion, and my mother disliked organ meats.

We also ate much fish: in summer, walleyed pike, bass, pickerel, crappies, and sunfish caught on poles made of trimmed tree branches; in winter, pickerel and pike hooked through the ice on special flagged rigs my dad carved out of apple-box wood. And there were suckers and red horse seined during the brief spring spawning season and "cured" in my uncle's smokehouse.

Twice a month we made cherry cakes with lard or bacon drippings, cocoa, and icings of powdered sugar mixed with heavy cream and colored with food coloring. Soft, raisin-filled cookies were a favorite. We ground the raisins in a heavy food grinder, the sort you anchor by tightening a large wing nut to the table. Most meals, though, did not include sweets, except for a slice of bread covered with jam or cream and sugar. We sometimes ate fresh strawberries, wild raspberries, lettuce, and fresh vegetables in season. During the winter, greens were entirely unavailable, even in the grocery stores.

Pancakes were a staple. The sourdough starter was months, possibly years, old, and bubbled away, sitting in its crock ("You Beat Eggs, We Beat Prices") on the kitchen range.

Dad was always first out of bed, winter or summer. He started the fire, building it from the quiescent coals of the night's banked fire. He flipped on the radio to WLS, and sounds of Roy Acuff, LuluBelle and Scottie, and Minnie Pearl wafted through the house as flames roared up the stovepipe.

Next, he fired the range, set the black fry pan and charred griddle over the heat, and added flour, a couple of fresh eggs, and water to his pancake batter. As bacon fried, he spooned grease onto the griddle and spread the batter. Upstairs, still in bed, I felt the rising warmth. A few inches from my face, frost melted and dripped from the nail ends.

I dressed quickly. Downstairs I piled griddlecakes on my plate and smeared them with fresh butter, clotted cream, and blueberry jam. Crisp bacon cut the sweetness. I drank fresh milk. Dad had coffee from a granite pot he kept brewing all day. He called the beverage "mud"; it was thicker than espresso. We never scoured the pot.

The Butchering

1

Dad told me to hold the knife and the pan.
I heard the click on wood
of the bullet inserted, rammed,
saw a flicker flash
in a tree beside the trough,
saw a grain in the sow's mouth,
felt my guts slosh.

"Stand back," Dad said.
Waffled snow track
pressed by his boots and mine.
Blood and foam.
"Keep the knife sharp, son,
and hold the pan."
One of us had shuffled,
tramped a design,
feet near the jack pine.
"She'll bleed slow.
Catch all the blood you can."

A rose unfolded, froze.
"Can't we wait?" I said.
"It should turn warmer."

Spark, spark buzzing
in the dark.

"It's time," Dad said, and waited.

2

Bless all this beauty! preacher
had exclaimed; *all sin and beauty
in this world, beast and innocent.*

Fistbones gripped the foreshortened
pulpit rim.
Thick glasses drove
his furious pupils in.

3

Dad brought the rifle to the skull.
The sow's nose plunged into the swill,
the tips of her white tallow ears as well.
Splunk! Straight through the brain, suet
and shell. Stunned! Discharge of food,
bran. Twitch of an ear. Potato, carrot,
turnip slab. "Quick. The knife, the pan."

He sliced the throat.
The eye closed over.
Hairy ears stood up, collapsed.
Her blood soured into gelatin.
She had begun to shit.

4

We dragged her
to the block-and-tackle rig.
We tied her tendons, raised her,

sloshed her up and down.
We shaved her hair,
spun her around, cut off
her feet and knuckles,
hacked off her head,
slashed her belly
from asshole down through
bleached fat throat.
Jewels spilled out,
crotches of arteries,
fluids danced and ran.

We hoisted her out of dog reach,
dumped her entrails in the snow,
left the head for the dogs to eat—
my mother disliked head meat.
The liver, steaming, monochrome,
quivered with eyes.
We took it home.

5

I went to my room.
Tongues licked my neck.
I spread my arms,
threw back my head.
The tendons of a heel snapped.
What had I lost?
bit, bridle, rage?

Preacher in his pulpit
fiddling, vestments aflame.
He, blazing, stepping down to me.
Hot piss came.
I knelt on the floor,
bent over, head in arms.
Piss washed down, more.
I clasped my loins,
arm crossed over arm.

And I cried
loving my guts,
O vulnerable guts,
guts of creatures.

The Sow's Head

The day was like pewter.
The gray lake a coat
open at the throat. The border
of trees — frayed mantle collar,
hairs, evergreen. The sky dun.
Chilling breeze. Hem of winter.

I passed the iodine-colored brook,
hard waters open,
the weight of the sow's head
an ache from shoulder to waist,
the crook of my elbow numb,
juices seeping through
the wrapping paper.

I was wrong to take it.
There were meals in it.
I would, Dad said, assist
with slaughter, scrape off
hair, gather blood.
I would be whipped for
thieving from the dogs.

I crossed ice
that shivered, shone.
No heads below, none;
nor groans — only water, deep,
and the mud beds of frogs asleep
not a bush quivered,
not a stone. Snow.

Old snow had formed
hard swirls, bone
and planes with
windwhipped ridges
for walking upon;
and beneath, in the deep,
bass quiet, perch whirling
fins, bluegills, sunfish,
dim-eyed soaking heat.
Mud would be soft down there,
rich, tan, deeper than a man:
silt of leeches, leaves
tumbling in from trees,
loon feces, mulch-thick
mudquick, and lignite forming,
cells rumbling, rifts.

I knelt, chopped through
layers of ice until
water, pus, spilled up
choking the wound. I widened
the gash. Tchick! Tchick!
Chips of ice flew.
Water blew from the hole,
the well, a whale, expired.
My knees were stuck to the ice.

I unwrapped the paper.
The head appeared
shorn of its beard.
Its ears stood up, the snout
with its Tinkertoy holes
held blood. Its eyes were shut.
There was grain on its mouth.

It sat on the snow
as though it lived below,
leviathan come for air,

limbs and hulk
dumb to my presence there.

I raised the sow's head
by its ears. I held it
over the hole, let it go,
watched it sink, a glimmer
of pink, a wink of a match,
an eyelid.
A bone in my side beat.

Snaring Rabbits

Snowshoe rabbits were in great abundance. Resting places
below flaring spruce trees were rich with droppings. Rabbit
trails compacted the snow, creating banks. Dad showed me
how to fashion picture-frame wire into a noose that would
slip easily around a rabbit's throat.

I tied several snares to overhanging branches. Rabbits
were smart, so I made the loop of wire big enough not to be
seen.

For a week, nothing. Two snares were brushed aside. The
others revealed no signs of rabbits, yet the trails were
freshly used.

Finally, I dismantled the traps. One snare held snowshoe
rabbit remains. There were signs of struggle, as though the
death had been difficult. I freed the snare and swung it,
still affixed to a frozen head, as far as I could into the
swamp.

Venison

Dad hunted alone. Other men preferred groups, posting
hunters at strategic spots on deer runs, assigning others as

beaters circling the forests, clattering, frightening the animals, driving them in toward the waiting hunters.

Deer season always began at dawn. Dad ate a hearty breakfast and packed a lunch. Over his union suit he wore a wool shirt, a sheepskin undervest, woolen pants, two pairs of wool socks, gum-soled boots, leather gloves with insert linings, and a mackinaw cap with ear flaps. He took his favorite Springfield rifle, not the most accurate of guns. He seldom drove to a hunting ground, preferring to tramp back through the snow, often waist-deep, to the swamps where he had earlier observed deer.

Why didn't I hunt with him? Any father would have delighted in the company of a tall, strong son, and I was already over 6'. He never chided me for my fear of guns or for my exaggerated sensitivity to killing. Later, I could laugh, saying that the only thing I ever shot was a bumblebee inside a morning glory — I would stick the barrel of my .22 rifle in on top of the bee and fire. My efforts at killing squirrels were always misses. I would level my gun, pull the trigger, and flinch, dismayed by a puff of dirt behind my intended victim, who sat there chattering.

Each day Dad spent in the woods seemed interminable. Would he shoot himself, or be killed by a bear? By twilight, as sunset stained the rich snow cover and dark was about to fall, my anxieties grew.

When Dad bagged a deer, he gutted it where he shot it and then dragged it through snowy thickets to a copse near Sundsteen Road. Then he walked home, cranked up the Model T, drove to the spot, draped the gutted deer over the hood, and drove back home.

First he sawed off the antlers; then he hacked off the head, which he threw outside for Fido, the dog. He flayed the hide. Later, it would go to a tannery, in exchange for pairs of gloves. We loved watching. Large pieces of venison he hung outside from an upright frame used for gutting and butchering. We would boil the ribs smothered in sauerkraut. Tougher, less-choice portions became hamburger.

Much of the meat we wrapped in newspaper and stored on the kitchen roof. Occasionally, Dad killed a second deer, usually a doe. This one Mother canned. The meat lasted until early summer.

Christmas Tree

Wednesday morning, December 20th. Shimmering trees were loaded with ice. My sister and I were dressed for the outdoors. "Get one with a good shape," my mother said. "And be careful with that axe."

We rushed on skis over the packed trail, crossing fields, the south pasture, and on through birch and tamarack to the lake. Fresh rabbit tracks had broken the ice crust. I carried the axe. We whirred along for half an hour and then we halted before a superb view of frozen Minnow Lake.

I shook a tree, a flaring spruce, freeing it of snow. It chopped easily. I tied a rope around it and secured the rope to my waist. "OK," I said. "You lead, Margie." The tree slid easily over the ski trail. We are exhilarated — cutting the tree was the first event of Christmas.

I built a clumsy stand in the living room, away from the heater. The odor of crushed needles, saps, and resins was magnificent.

We had few ornaments: Of a dozen glass pieces, my favorites were a pair of multicolored, miniature bass viols, and a small glass deer, missing its antlers. We made chains from the colored pages of old magazines glued with paste made of flour, water, and salt. I enjoyed fitting the pink and red twisted wax candles in their metal holders to the branches. We lighted the candles.

We drew pictures for one another, to keep secret until Christmas morning. We had made presents for our mother: I decorated a box of safety matches with fancy paper taken from envelopes supplied by our teacher, and I carved a bar of Ivory soap into a squirrel. Miss Crocker sketched the animal, and I was near tears before I managed to whittle the creature free of the soap. Around its neck I tied a small bit of green ribbon and a medallion saying Squirrel. I hoped my mother would like it.

The Christmas Program

For three weeks, on wintry afternoons, huddled near the heating stove, we rehearsed the Christmas Program. Each of us had an individual recitation: Most were short winter or Christmas bits with humorous twists. We recited "'Twas the Night Before Christmas" in unison. Paper snowflakes covered the windows. The tree was decorated with homemade ornaments: flashing tops from condensed milk cans, tiny crosses covered with gum-wrapper tin foil, Santa Claus heads, feeble attempts at reindeers, crayola renditions of balls, dolls, books. And, of course, the ubiquitous colored paper chains, with strings of popcorn.

My assignment was to memorize vast chunks of "Christmas in Other Lands" from an encyclopedia. I started memorizing in November. I copied out the text by hand and carried sheaves of paper, memorizing at odd moments. I recited while pumping water. We made cuts in my piece.

We strung hay wire across the end of the schoolroom and hung white bed sheets. Presents for Miss Crocker, mostly handkerchiefs and cheap perfume, lay beneath the tree. Tiny paper bags, mysterious in their contents, were also there. We were promised a Santa. (The real St. Nick couldn't visit all the schools in the world.) We agreed to spend no more than a quarter on gifts and prayed that the Jollys wouldn't draw our names. They were the poorest family, and whatever they gave would be soiled. I bought jacks for Osmo Makinnen.

The performance started at 7:30. Miss Crocker arrived

early. Families walked to school. There was a startling display of the aurora borealis. The air hovered near zero. We dressed warmly, and the walk, which took half an hour, was festive. Excited kids ran back and forth behind their parents, using far more energy than the walk required.

Despite some problems with the bed sheets, the program went well. I appeared halfway through, reciting facts about Christmas in other lands. That I was a bore never entered my head, despite the restlessness of the audience. Most of the men hung to the rear, behind the women. I concluded with Norway. The applause was brief. Holding lighted candles, the school sang "The Night Before Christmas" and "Silent Night."

Jingling bells heralded the entrance of the old soul who was bewhiskered with cotton batting and wore a dime-store suit. He made his way to the front where a couple of kids were sniveling. He inquired of our behavior, gave his ho hos, and presented us with candy canes. My suspicions were confirmed—this was not Santa but my cousin Albert. I recognized his throat, and I recognized his boots—black leather with buckles resembling silver harps.

Christmas Morning

It was 6:30 A.M. A drear, metallic sun soaked the heavy frost on the window glass. The fire downstairs was out. Dad wouldn't be up early on a holiday.

Unable to contain ourselves, we threw our clothes over our union suits and rushed downstairs. Nothing seemed changed—if Santa had come, there was no special magic, no special scent in the air. My sisters reached the living room first.

Our stockings were full, and kitchen chairs had been pulled close to the tree and piled with gifts. From Santa, Margie got a doll, a coloring book and crayolas, underwear, socks, and a gingham dress with Bo Peeps on the skirt. Nell's gifts were similar. Everett received a wooden train, skis, and clothes. My presents were a coloring book and crayolas; a picture book of Robert Louis Stevenson's poems; a set of iron-on transfers of Maggie and Jiggs, Popeye and Olive Oyl, Tillie the Toiler, and Mutt and Jeff; wool socks; cotton underwear; school shirts; Old Maid cards; and a small pinball game, pocket-sized, my favorite gift, one I would play throughout the year, inventing elaborate scoring games.

Our stockings were stuffed with an orange, an apple, walnuts, hard ribbon candy, and a Big Little Book. Mine was *Tarzan of the Apes*. I loved these books. They cost a nickel. The drawings were as fascinating as the text. Margie's was *Little Women*. The raisin-filled cookies we left for Santa were untouched. And we saw Sears labels in our clothes. Nell's dress still had a price tag — $1.95.

Dad soon had the fire going. We settled down on the braided rug and began to color. The pristine pages were inviting, and placing the first tints was fun. We rushed to finish a picture. Mine was of a chubby straw-hatted boy with a fishing pole. Margie chose a girl in a pinafore pouring tea for dolls. At first, I stayed within the lines; then I got bored — the spaces for coloring are vast and empty. There were no hints that you could mix colors or try for shading and nuance. If this Christmas ran true, by afternoon the books would be tossed into our toy boxes, seldom to be fingered again. Then Dad surprised me with an air rifle, a gift I didn't want, and showed me how to insert a bullet and squeeze the trigger. "We'll shoot a hen for supper," he said.

Killing the Hen

Old Crip danced on spurless legs, making deep-maw proprietary sounds. Once the hens were eating corn and chortling, he fed himself, keeping a wary eye on us.

We selected a large Rhode Island Red, one no longer laying. "Now," Dad said. "Point the barrel at her eye; then pull the trigger slow."

An olio of feelings: I did not want to shoot. I did not want to displease Dad. Oblivious, the hen pecked at her corn.

The trigger felt like ice. My index finger seemed jointless.

"Now, do it right," Dad warned.

The bird's yellowish ear was a minuscule sun. Stunned, she chortled, rattled, and fell, clawed the air, stiffened, and then stilled. Dad whipped out a pocketknife and slit her throat. "Wasn't too bad, was it?" He lifted the hen by its legs. "Nice fat one. Be good with dumplin's."

I plunged the bird into boiling water. The feathers loosened immediately and smelled like rancid rags. Then came the singeing and butchering. Mom planned an early supper, complete with blueberry pie, from berries picked the previous summer.

The afternoon was lazy. Margie and I skied for an hour, returning to a kitchen fragrant with delicious steam. The yellow dumpling dough, rich with hen fat, was nearly ready. Dad was napping. We settled near the tree, ate candy, and read the Hearst funnies: "The Katzenjammer Kids," "Blondie," "Gasoline Alley," and "Maggie and Jiggs." Dad decided to milk Lady early, before supper, so that we could enjoy a long evening.

Supper was superb! The dumplings were sweet. The hen, despite her age, was tender. We quarreled as usual over the wishbone. Margie won, but refused to break the bone, saying she'd wrap it in tinfoil and keep it near her bed for good luck — the Christmas wishbone. Mashed potatoes, chicken, and gravy. Canned, cut green beans. And canned blueberry pie! We ate a whole quarter of a pie apiece. Dad smoked a rare cigar. Margie, Mom, and I played Old Maid. I stayed up after everyone was in bed, sat near the tree, and stared at the candles. I blew them out and went to bed, where I read chapters from Luke. I snuggled down against

the encroaching cold. The downstairs fire settled into
cinders.

Ice-Fishing

Dad, Charlie Mattek, and I packed sandwiches and drove
down Sundsteen Road as far as it went, disappearing into a
spruce and tamarack forest. I wore extra woolen socks—
comfort for a full day on the ice.

For an hour we tramped through highland, finally
reaching a large cranberry marsh. Despite the intense cold,
some of the marsh was unfrozen. Dad led the way. I
brought up the rear, carrying a gunny sack with lines and
food. A dour metallic tone concealed the sky and a ridge of
firs across Columbus Lake seemed remote and desolate. A
brace of partridge, interrupted picking dead seeds from
bushes, scurried clumsily through the snow and into flight.
Rabbit and deer trails crossed and intersected, marked by
shiny black droppings. An occasional jay screamed.

Despite a heavy orthopedic boot and a knee brace,
Charlie was a good walker. As a boy he had had polio. He
was in his mid-twenties, of moderate height, with a handsome hewn face and white teeth. His hair and eyes were
brown. He loved fishing. He and Dad played music weekends at local dances. Charlie had a good but untrained
voice and played guitar.

We chopped half a dozen spruce and dragged them onto
the ice, as a windbreak and for firewood. The lake surface
was rough, as though it had melted recently and then
quickly frozen. Ice hummocks provided traction. Rarely
were any of the thousand regional lakes ice-slick, free of
snow, and suitable for skating. We set up camp about a
hundred yards from shore. No other fishermen were in
sight.

Dad and Charlie chopped through the foot-thick ice. Yellowish water, pickerel-colored, welled up. By careful chipping, the holes were widened, and, with a scoop — a piece of window screen nailed to a birch stick — we removed ice chips. Next, we embedded birch saplings, one per hole, some three feet back from the hole. Each sapling, angled, supported a line. Dad had carved small fish forms from apple-box wood and inserted the line first through a hole in the tail of the form and then through a second hole in the head so that the wooden fish rode free, more or less parallel to the ice. When a fish hit the salted minnow bait, the wooden fish tail flipped straight up in the air.

We set lines in threes. Mine were nearest the shelter; Dad's were further off, as were Charlie's. My job was to move around with the screen scoop keeping the holes free of new ice. We made a fire. The spruce sap flamed beautifully. I dried a soaked glove while Dad and Charlie made excursions for more wood. The supply would last until early evening, allowing us just enough light to make our way back to the car.

We melted snow in a large pail, added ground coffee, and hung it over the fire in the Y of an embedded branch. A delicious aroma of boiling coffee blended with spruce gum.

The fish bit well. We hoped for walleyes; they were the least bony and most delicious. We fished deep, but if the salted minnow rode too low, the pike wouldn't snag it. The trick was to drop the line until it curled. By drawing it up six inches and securing it, you positioned the bait. I set my lines at intervals, primarily for bass and pickerel.

Pickerel are notorious for giving test tugs on the line, eating off salted minnow, almost as if they know, avoiding the risk of the barbed hook. We crept to the hole, grabbed the line, and jiggled it to give the illusion that a minnow was escaping. Usually, when a pickerel strikes, if you yank fast on the line, you'll snag him. Once caught, it may still rip free. Whenever it slackens, you draw the line taut, and when you glimpse the snaky form, you jerk with all your might and bring it forth flopping and squirming. Its protective slime soon freezes. To spare the creature suffering, you strike its head with a knife, stunning it. Within minutes it freezes board-stiff.

The day's haul: six pickerel, four three-pound walleyes, fifteen large bluegills, and six perch. At 4:00 we threw the remaining wood on the fire, leaving one tree intact for other fishermen to use, packed our fish into gunny sacks, retrieved our gear, and started for home. I was tired but exhilarated. My feet were cold. In twenty minutes we were enjoying a supper of fresh beef, mashed potatoes, and fresh bread. After supper, Dad and I cleaned the fish, stowing them outside on the roof to freeze.

Harvesting Ice

In January, we tramped often through thigh-deep snow to Minnow Lake. A narrow but swift creek that flowed into the lake rarely froze. Traversing it was difficult. We threw down fallen tree trunks, crossed and came to the lake, which was frozen except for the area around the creek. I saw my uncle, cousins Jim and Frenchy, and their team of horses, Bill and Bess, out on the ice. We arrived in time for the first excavations of ice blocks, rectangular shapes formed by augers and saws. By inserting a special saw, resembling a crosscut with large teeth, one man worked along the cut, eventually freeing a block, which was then loaded onto an iceboat—a sledge converted to a sleigh by means of strategically placed tire irons. The blocks, all roughly three by six feet, would be halved and quartered later for storing in sawdust. Uncle Pete and Dad did the sawing. Frenchy and Jim, with some help from me, pushed the heavy blocks onto the iceboat. The whiteness of the blocks surprised me; the water itself, once the blocks were removed, was the color of iodine, stained by the leaf mulch. The lake was rumored to be bottomless — if you swam there and dove, all you would ever touch was mud, over six feet of it. We piled the ice blocks five high, a considerable load for the horses to draw up the steep incline to my uncle's farm. We stacked the ice neatly on the leeward side of the barn and then returned for other loads. We made three trips, and just before dusk we mulched the ice pile with straw and covered it with sawdust. So preserved, the ice would last through the summer. Our share of the ice — half a dozen huge blocks — we took home, Dad driving Uncle Pete's team. In hot weather the water would be pure for lemonade. As a special treat, we'd chip it, pack it with salt into a freezer, and make ice cream.

Part Two: Spring

Thaw

The first tentative thaw began in early March. By noon the sun warmed the accumulated snow and ice, forming small streams along the shoveled paths and on the gravel road where the plows had kept the snow layer minimal. Pebbles absorbed the wan sun, warming the adjacent snow. Snow loosened from fir trees and crashed to the ground. Ptarmigan and prairie hens were in evidence, losing their skittery temerity of humans and crowding close to the fowl yard. To find a resplendent pheasant cock feeding with the hens was common. For the first time since November the chickens had the run of the outdoor pen.

Rabbits and hares scampered over the snow. Maple sap dripped. Black bear emerged from hibernation, hungry and dangerous. For several nights, a she-bear lingered in our field, eating garbage. We kept near the house, alert for noise in the underbrush.

Ice on the lakes remained thick enough for fishing. The surfaces, however, were covered with slush, so we sealed our boots with tallow. We fished in Columbus Lake, where the game fish were, and not in Minnow with its swarms of fingerling perch — "rough" fish, tiny, filled with bones.

At school we were restless, anxious for the snow to fade, eager for the reappearance of flowers and birds. Though a few minuscule buds appeared on the willows, winter still held sway; in fact, we expected a blizzard as late as early April. These were my last weeks of school before starting high school in the fall.

The delay of spring exacerbated our restlessness. Reading was difficult. I paced my chores, took twice as long as usual to clean the barn, to milk, to fill woodboxes. I wouldn't shed long underwear until Memorial Day, that magical day when there was a whiff of summer and you could swim, although the lakes remained bone-chillingly cold. The stench of soiled wool, stale long johns, and unwashed bodies permeated school and home, the latter chinked and weather-stripped against the cold for so many months.

Bathing

The ritual Saturday night baths were always easiest in warm weather. We heated water on the woodstove — filling the copper boiler was my chore — then dumped it into a galvanized tub. Mom arranged a spot near the kitchen range, draping blankets over chairs for privacy.

My brother Everett, my sister Margie, and I drew straws for the first bath. The longest straw went first; the shortest bathed in the water used by the other two. There was always fussing as we scooped off the gray soapy scum (we called it "dirt"). Not until puberty did I enjoy my own bathwater. We used Ivory soap most of the time and, for a special treat, Lifebuoy. We believed the ads: Lifebuoy prolonged our lives. Certainly, the odor was astringent. Ivory, on the other hand, because of its reputed purity (wasn't it 99 and 44/100 percent pure?) appealed to my mother. Once we kids were bathed, Mom bathed in fresh water. She lingered in her bath while Dad waited to take his.

Always the crude one, Dad bathed only when Mom insisted. "Dirty Old Pup" was her epithet for him, delivered not entirely without love. My mother washed his back. Then he toweled himself singing.

Spring Housecleaning

We hung bedding on clotheslines. We placed mattresses on old newspapers and checked for ticks and bedbugs. If there were infestations, eggs dormant during the winter would soon hatch. We were usually free of vermin. Where did bedbugs come from? From Welfare? From a visitor? One spring my brother and I were viciously bitten. Dad mixed kerosene and creosote and sprayed our mattress with a Fly-Tox sprayer, soaking the areas infested with eggs. Fortunately, the creatures did not spread to the other beds that year.

Once Miss Crocker found lice on our scalps and sent us home with a note. Mom washed our heads with creosote cut with a small amount of kerosene, careful not to get it in our eyes. None of us liked the noisome odor, but knew there was no other way to rid ourselves. After a good shampooing, Mom combed dead lice and eggs from our hair. Two such treatments were required. To have lice was a terrible stigma; you were "dirty." Spring, alas, brought onslaughts of other vermin, including mice and rats.

Spring was also the time for new linoleum. For greater insulation, the new coverings went right over the old. The aroma of varnish and petroleum filled the house. We soaked our hooked rugs in soap and water. My job was to wring them out. The frayed ones we took apart, saving the cloth strips for hooking more rugs. One of the last chores was washing the windows with a mixture of hot water and vinegar.

Redhorse Run

The redhorse, a scavenger fish related to the carp, spawned in late March. Only then, in those ice-cold flowages, was redhorse edible. Fortunately, the fish inhabited very few lakes. They were bottom-feeders; their large hinged mouths scooped up mud, sifting out whatever debris — carrion, leaves — was edible. In shallower lakes the water grew so muddy that game fish died, or migrated elsewhere on the Chain of Lakes free of scavengers.

For taking redhorse, Dad fashioned a spear of three spiked nails driven through a birch pole that had been smoothed to bare wood. He angled the nails to give the effect of Triton's spear and then filed the nails to sharp points, fashioning a small barb above each point to secure the struck fish.

Only two more hours of daylight: Redhorse ran best late in the day. We parked in a grassy area above the fast-moving water. Against the sandy bottom, meandering fish were visible. Some waited in place, depositing roe. My uncle had already arrived. I heard my cousins' voices upstream. The horizon was utterly blue, with a hint of a salmon tint from the setting sun. In the distance rose a pair of pine-covered hills. Honking Canada geese flew north to nesting areas.

The stream was about two feet deep, with the occasional deeper pockets preferred by largemouth bass. Dad told me to bring the gunny sacks.

He speared from shore. When he flung a fish on the grass, its weight tore it from the spear barbs. Although the water was icy, Dad decided he'd wade in for better luck. When he began to lose feeling in his toes, he came out and massaged his feet. Then he returned to the water. The fish, frenzied to spawn, kept coming. In less than an hour I had filled three gunny sacks. We strung more fish on clothesline rope.

Dad dried his feet and put on his shoes, and, after dumping the fish into the car, we set off to find my uncle. They had filled a dozen gunny sacks. The redhorse had never been so prolific.

That night we scaled, gutted, and filleted the fish, which we smoked in my uncle's smokehouse. In exchange, we kept the fires going. The best-tasting fish required a week's smoking.

I loved this plenitude: There were more fish than we could eat. And smoked fish kept indefinitely. "Redhorse eat drowned people," my mother said. We devoured the fish cold, boiled, fried—in casseroles and sandwiches and with sourdough pancakes.

That we might starve was a common fear. Counting on relatives was difficult. Though my uncle had a larger and richer farm than ours, his selfish wife, Kate, rarely shared their largesse. The burden on Dad of keeping us supplied with food was immense. If there was no money for meat, if the Welfare supplies ran out, there was only one alternative—hunt and fish. He worried particularly in early spring when our potatoes and carrots had gone soft, sprouting in the root cellar. But soon Lady would have fresh grass for pasture, her milk would turn sweet, and she would drop a new calf. And our vegetable garden would grow.

Homemade Ice Cream

With ice pick and hammer we chipped ice from deposits near the pump. When a gunny sack was full, we smashed the bag broadside with the hammer to crush the ice for our single-quart hand freezer. Mom prepared a mixture of canned blueberries—our favorite—or of fresh or canned strawberries, cream, sugar, vanilla, and beaten egg, dumped it into the can, inserted the dasher, and placed the whole into the wooden freezer, securing the crank top. We packed the ice loosely, alternating layers with salt. After nearly an hour of churning, the ice cream was set. The person who cranked the mixture got to lick the dasher for an extra serving.

Trailing Arbutus

The pink and white flowers of the rare trailing arbutus, indigenous to a few of the northernmost regions of the United States, exuded a special fragrance. Peeping forth from patches of snow, they seemed pure. The rarest blooms were tinged with lavender.

My sister and I made morning excursions for the flowers, shaped them into small bouquets, packed them with wet starflower moss, wrapped the moss in waxed paper, and filled two oblong cake pans with them. At 6 P.M. Dad drove us to the railway station. The train from Milwaukee, bringing fishermen and tourists, arrived at 6:30.

Margie and I positioned ourselves on the platform where most of the passengers detrained. We were shy, and I felt more than a tinge of self-pity for our poverty. Since I found it difficult to ask for a sale, I positioned myself in front of a potential customer and held up some arbutus, mumbling, "ten cents." For large bouquets we asked a quarter. The selling took less than an hour; by that time the train had moved on toward Land O'Lakes. We sold about half of our flowers, making slightly over a dollar apiece. The remaining bouquets we hawked in various stores along Main Street. My dad, easily affronted, took it as a personal insult when a storekeeper refused to buy. We enjoyed a good season if we cleared $20. Except for an occasional fifty cents for a movie at the Vilas Theater, we saved the money in a tomato juice can for fall school clothes.

The Radio

Our Sears, Roebuck Silvertone operated on storage batteries. We were so far from the transmitters in Chicago and

Milwaukee that reception, except for early mornings and after dark, was filled with static. The radio, covered with a crocheted doily in a pineapple pattern, sat on a shelf above our dining table.

"Stella Dallas" was my mother's favorite program. Every morning, Dad tuned to WLS, "The Prairie Farmer Station," for the country music stars. Evenings we heard "I Love a Mystery" and "Amos and Andy." My favorite comedian was Fred Allen. I despised George and Gracie and found Jack Benny only marginally funny. I rarely found "The Lone Ranger" or "Jack Armstrong" absorbing. Our Saturday ritual: Dad bought peanuts in the shell and the Sunday Milwaukee *Sentinel*. We were on our honor not to read the comics until dark. Then out came the peanuts and paper, and on went the radio. My program was "The Hit Parade." For an entire year I kept meticulous records of all the top songs, awarding elaborate percentages, so that on December 31st I would know the year's winners. My statistics were pointless, however, for on the final Saturday of the year the program featured its own rundown of the top songs.

Religion

Two persons influenced my religious beliefs: Mrs. Ohlson and Adeline Mattek. Mrs. Ohlson arrived early that spring with two teenagers, Fern and Russell, and convinced Dad to let her refurbish a dilapidated shack we had on our property. She had separated from her husband, Harry, a fellow WPA worker on my dad's road-building crew. Harry, in fact, first broached the subject with Dad, saying that he would stay in town in a room but that he couldn't afford to rent both a house for his family and a room for himself. Dad agreed to help this mild-natured man, and on one weekend Dad, Harry, and Russell erected a shack of poplar poles just a stone's throw from our house.

Through that summer Mrs. Ohlson sunbathed in bra and panties, displaying herself on an old army cot. Her teenagers found work in town, so the entire day was hers. She was in her late forties and had sagging bosoms and a floppy stomach. Her hair was done up in tightly rolled curlers. She was often tipsy.

Margie and I would sneak up on her, hiding, making animal sounds and throwing pebbles on her roof. Mrs. Ohlson would scream that she knew who we were and then lie back quietly on her cot.

On one occasion she caught us red-handed; and when she challenged us, clad in her usual scanty fashion, Margie ran off while I stayed to face her.

She motioned for me to sit. "I don't hurt you," she began. "Why do you hurt me?" I had no answer. She brought cookies from the house and then began to talk about God, extolling a "personal relationship" with Jesus as her lodestone. She asked me if I had been baptized. I said I had never been to church.

She picked up the Milwaukee *Sentinel*. "Here." She pointed to an article on the "Imminent End of the World." A sect in Mattoon, Illinois, her home town, had given away all their earthly goods and was planning to sit on their church roof at midnight on May 15th, Armageddon Day, to be assumed directly into heaven. "If they're right," Mrs. Ohlson said, "since I've been baptized, I'll go to heaven. But you and your family will never get there. You're heathens." She depicted hell in frighteningly vivid terms.

During the next weeks, Mrs. Ohlson seemed obsessed with Armageddon; her newspaper carried even more features on the heralding sect. My parents declared Mrs. Ohlson "bonkers." That's why Harry had left her. Whether you go to heaven, my dad insisted, depends not on your being sprinkled with preacher water but rather on your conscience. God doesn't care about churches; He cares about your soul. You don't need mumbo jumbo. My mother's views were conditioned by her views of social inequity. If we did attend church, she felt, our clothes would betray us. The townsfolk would be condescending. Such attitudes, she insisted, had nothing to do with God. All are equal in His sight. If you wore a grass skirt, painted your rear end with varnish to keep it warm, or dressed in the latest fashion, it was all the same to God.

May 15 was flawlessly clear, hot enough for a straw hat. By late afternoon, black clouds had formed; they lingered in the north, producing a brilliant sunset. Going to bed that night was a special ritual for me. Good-nights, embraces, kisses. I kept my apprehensions to myself and read the Bible — chapters dealing with Christ's arrest, crucifixion, and ascension. Shortly after midnight, winds and rain of cyclonic force shook the house with incredible lightning, thunder, and hailstones. I covered my head and prayed, sure that the house would be swept off, that we would all be killed. If only I were baptized!

The night passed. Several large trees near the road were uprooted. Heavy rain filled the swampy depressions below the house. The sky was sunny and windblown, the air fraught with a fresh chill. Mrs. Ohlson's predictions had not come true. I was not disappointed when the woman took herself and her children back to Matoon at the end of the summer.

*   *   *

Adeline Mattek seldom glanced at our house. No matter the weather, this remarkable girl, scarred with a harelip, never missed Saturday mass. On this particular morning there had been a deep snowfall. The county plow was not yet working. Adeline appeared wearing an ankle-length green wool coat, a knit scarf, and a large navy blue cap. She walked fast with her head down, which gave the illusion that she was about to fall on her face. Perhaps that was how she hid her harelip.

I had seen the inside of her home only once, when I stopped for a drink on my way to find Lady, who had strayed. An impression remains of two rooms, one filled with sagging beds and couches where Adeline, her four brothers and sister, and her parents slept. (One brother, Charlie, was the musician who fished with my dad and eventually married my North Dakota cousin Evelyn.) Gunny sacks had been sewn together and filled with straw for mattresses. Although Adeline, about seventeen, was the elder of the two daughters, she lingered in the background while her sister gave me milk to drink.

She had dropped out of school and now stayed home looking after her family. Her joy was her religion. Adeline puzzled me, and as my fear of hell grew, I grew obsessed, loving her with a platonic intensity.

As Easter neared, I read the Bible with increasing fervor. Whether I understood or not, each word was truth. Even the interminable "begat" verses were mines of spiritual ore. I meditated over the saccharine color prints of Jesus with lambs, of Jesus being scourged, of Jesus dying, and I began to talk to Jesus, shaping the air with my hands, imagining Him as my very own.

The circumstance resolving my struggle was my first ejaculation. I had no idea what had transpired. I woke during the night to find my belly wet. At first I thought it was blood. Without disturbing my brother, I crept from bed and found a flashlight. Where had the strange substance come from? My parents told me nothing of sexual change, and I was too naive to relate my own seminal flow to that of farm animals. My fevered psyche interpreted the incident as a warning from Jesus that I must be baptized.

I resolved to go to mass the next morning, Palm Sunday. My parents approved — though not without some hesitation that I might turn Catholic. I waited for Adeline to walk past before setting out myself. I hoped to remain anonymous, so I decided to attend a later mass.

I dallied along the road, examining pools for frogs' eggs, throwing sticks and stones into a swirl of rusty water emerging through a culvert near Mud Creek, and admiring a grove of juneberry trees loaded with blossoms. Twice I turned and started back for home.

By the time I reached St. Joseph's Catholic Church, the second mass had ended, and there was no other. Jesus, I felt, had arranged this timing for some umbrageous reason of His own, sheltering me from Catholicism. Services were about to begin at the Christ Evangelical Church across the street. On the steps were Eileen Ewald and her parents. I had had a crush on Eileen ever since she appeared in second grade and said "sugar." It was not the word itself, but her cultured tone in saying it that struck me as special. I ached to be in love with her.

I followed Eileen into the church and sat in a pew at the very back. I was entranced by the pale oak altar with its pastel plaster crucifixion. The organ music, the first I had ever heard, was splendid. All through the sermon, by the Reverend Joseph Krubsack, I sat in a daze. Jesus had directed me here!

I lingered until Rev. Krubsack was alone and told him of my wish for baptism. He promised to baptize me and my family on the Sunday after Easter. But I would not become a full Lutheran, he warned, until I had passed Instruction.

Easter

My faith in Santa Claus and the Easter Rabbit disappeared when I was eleven. I had seen oranges in the box of groceries Dad brought home. We never had oranges except at Christmas, and Santa usually brought them, putting some in stockings and leaving the rest on the table. "Stay up tonight and see," Dad said.

Margie and Nell went to bed early, anticipating sugar-
plum visions and reindeer hooves. I yawned and said I was
sleepy, too. Dad was listening to some boxing match. "No
you don't," he laughed. "You stay up with us."

When the boxing ended, Mom brought out toys and
fruit. We stuffed stockings and placed the toys in strategic
spots for easy discovery. Considerately, my parents did not
deprive me of all surprise — they put out my gifts when I
was in bed.

Easter was always easier than Christmas, less a matter of
deportment than of colored eggs and chocolate. We tinted
the eggs on Saturday, using Paas dyes and decal transfers.
That evening Margie and I hid eggs outside, creating elaborate maps for finding them, one map per egg. Margie hid
mine and I hid hers. We included our parents, fashioning
the most complex hunt for Dad. Easter morning was chilly
but sunny. My father refused to participate, despite our
fussing and pleading. When we found them, all of the eggs
were cracked and frozen.

On Easter mornings we visited Mrs. Kula. She had sent
an invitation via her daughter Celia to visit her. She
appeared at her door wearing a white babushka. Since she
spoke no English, she smiled and waved us inside, where
she gave us two brightly colored eggs and a few jelly beans.
She did not wish us to linger, for she soon opened the door,
bowed, and smiled us out. Years later, one of her daughters
said that her mother's ritual was an ancient peasant one: If
you could inveigle a non-Catholic, a non-Pole, to receive
gifts on Easter morning, that person would be your
scapegoat, carrying away your entire year's burden of sins.
We were oblivious to these subtleties.

Ploughing and Seeding

For five dollars, my uncle hired out his team, Bill and Bess,
for plowing. I was a coward near horses, and when Dad

asked me to drive the team while he steered the plow I refused. Horses would suddenly shake their necks and bare their teeth.

My uncle was a hard driver. I had seen him beat Bill with a club while the horse was tied in his stall. In pain, the horse broke free and ran from the barn toward Minnow Lake, with my uncle in pursuit. I followed and saw him corner Bill, who waited docilely while my uncle, his wrath spent, grabbed the broken halter and stroked Bill's neck with surprising gentleness.

Eruptions of violence always dismayed me. In a recurring dream, Osmo Makinnen threatened to attack. When I sought to defend myself, my arms froze at my sides. Usually I woke in a sweat. Why my impotence? Dad had given me pointers — and he had boxed at carnivals. To support my ineptitude, I found the Bible useful. If you followed Christ's example, you simply turned the other cheek. I found the violence of men far worse than any violence of horses. A man enraged by a horse unleashed an enormous force few men could hope to restrain.

One lasting image is of my father beating Lady. I had been told to graze her in timothy along Sundsteen Road. Since she was always docile, I went to the house for a drink of water and lingered talking to Margie. When I returned, Lady was not where I had left her. Shortly, I heard my dad's angry voice — the cow was in the cornfield. When he flung stones at Lady, she sped crazily across the potato field. Dad cornered her near a fence, grabbed a tree branch, and beat her. She stumbled and fell, quivering, her belly swollen with calf. I grabbed the branch. Dad was shaking with rage. I flung my arms around Lady's neck. I felt her blood on my face. Slowly, she righted herself. I told Dad it was my fault. "It's all right," Dad said. "Take her to the barn. Give her water."

There didn't seem to be much Dad couldn't do. Before plowing, he loaded a stoneboat with cow manure and

spread it over the field. He emptied the outhouse, reserving the rich human ordure for the garden plots. He joked,
saying he could tell the Saturday night deposits by the
peanuts.

He plowed with immense skill, working the plow blades
into the loam and guiding the horses with their lead har-
ness around his shoulders. Margie, Everett, and I followed,
plucking earthworms from the moist turned-over soil. We'd
use them for fishing. Dad plowed the large field first, where
potatoes, corn, and squash grew. The small field held our
other crops: tomatoes, cabbage, Swiss chard, onions, green
beans, and peas. The plowing went smoothly. We had
cleared all large rocks from the field, and apart from one
obstinate huge pine stump, the areas were free of obstacles.
Dad disked the soil and then leveled it with a drag. By late
afternoon, he had finished.

My mother and Margie had prepared potatoes for plant-
ing, slicing them into bits, each with an eye for a new plant.
White potatoes kept better than reds, although the latter
matured faster. We planted the potato bits and corn seeds
with a special gadget, a metal flanged cup on a long handle.
You dropped a potato or grain of corn into the cup, thrust
the cup into the soil, and moved the handle towards you,
opening the jaws of the cup and releasing the seed. On you
moved, a foot and a half or so, for the next hill. Every tenth
hill of corn, you mixed in a few pumpkin or squash seeds.

Burning Brush

When we cut firewood in the fall, we threw the lopped
branches into piles for spring burning, to lessen the fire
hazard of dead scattered brush. In the spring, we trimmed
the birch grove on the hill behind the house, picking up
debris downed during the winter and adding to the piles.

Wherever these brush piles burned, raspberry bushes sprang up.

Birth

The Poland China sow's pregnancy was only evident a few days before she birthed piglets. We had no sure way of telling when she'd been in heat. She was always with the boar until late winter, when we butchered him. The pig shed was near the barn. Like the other outbuildings, it was of scrap pine covered with tar paper, and was just large enough to accommodate two grown pigs. During cold weather, we crammed it with straw. Weather permitting, the animals slept outside, snuggled into the pits they had dug with their snouts, searching for edible roots. The yard was well fenced, with wire mesh buried in the ground to make excavating difficult for the pigs. Late each spring, once the sow had birthed, we moved the pen to a freshly cleared area plentiful with roots. The pigs would work for us, tilling and fertilizing the soil.

Late one afternoon, returning from the lake, I noticed the sow on her side making gurgling sounds. She lay with her face half buried in mud and her foaming mouth open. Her one visible eye was closed and wet. Her vagina was inflamed and swollen. Soon a piglet oozed forth wearing a purplish semitransparent placental shroud. I had never before seen pigs born. When the second one dropped, I ran to the house for my mother.

Five more piglets emerged. Since sows are notorious for mistaking their farrow for placentas and are apt to devour an entire litter, we had to act fast. I grabbed a stick, ready to drive off the sow. We threw armfuls of straw into the pen, near the shed, hoping to entice her to where it was dry. It worked. The farrow soon found her teats and were feeding. When the piglets matured, we sold some, traded others

for hay, and kept two, a boar and a sow, for the next year's
breeding.

*   *   *

Two weeks after the birth of the pigs, Lady dropped
another bull calf. We had recorded the date of her visit to
Mattek's bull, so we were sure of her due time. That morning she was restless when I led her, lowing softly, to a
clearing of luxuriant timothy. I checked on her at noon.
She was eating, and all seemed in order.

At about 4 P.M., I was startled by her lowing and saw her
hunched, standing with her legs spread at odd angles. I
ran to the field. She was straining to drop the calf, visible
now up to its shoulders. She kept gazing at her rear, looked
stricken, and moved in vague slow circles, as if to ease her
pain. Then she lay down on her side, panting, her muscles
pushing to expel the calf. I knelt, grabbed the calf's wet
head, and drew it toward me. The shoulders pushed clear,
and the hind portions slipped forth. With a jackknife I
severed the umbilical chord. Blood. As soon as the calf
could stand, Lady rose, turned, and started licking it.
"Quick," Mom said. "Get the pitchfork."

When I returned, the calf was already feeding. A huge
placental mass, iridescent, resembling a great sea slug,
exuded from Lady's vagina. It could have filled a washtub. I
speared it with the pitchfork and threw it over the fence. If
Lady had eaten it, her milk would have soured for a
month.

Memorial Day

The county's two commemorative days were Memorial Day
and the Fourth of July. The former began at 10 A.M. with a
parade led by members of the American Legion, the high

school band, the Legion Women's Auxiliary, and a scattering of town dignitaries in automobiles. Paper poppies, in
honor of the vets who had died on Flanders Field, sprouted
in buttonholes. To be sure of a vantage spot near the depot,
we arrived at nine. My sister wore a flowered dress Mom
had made on her treadle sewing machine. My dad, my
brother, and I wore new Sears shirts. We were promised ice
cream cones at Zimplemann's Parlor, an enterprise run by a
domineering old German and three plump unmarried
daughters. To the rear of the parlor was a violin in a glass
case, which played, via mechanical fingers after you inserted a dime, a limited repertory — two or three Strauss
waltzes and a few sentimental American love songs by
Carrie Jacobs Bond.

Promptly at 11:00, the hour of the Armistice ending
World War I, Dr. McMurray flew over in a red biplane and
dropped a wreath of poppies into Eagle River, near the
iron bridge. McMurray was a physician of doubtful creden-
tials. If one could, one chose Dr. Oldfield, the only other
doctor in town. McMurray drank too much and loved
regaling his patients with his reputed feats as a war ace in
France.

Occasionally, flowers drifted free of the wreath and
floated out over the crowd. Catching one brought good
luck. Later, after Fred Draeger, the district attorney, delivered the Decoration Day speech, everybody marched to the
cemetery, led by the Legion, the band, and the dignitaries.
An honor guard fired off salutes.

Two of my mother's brothers had been gassed in the
trenches, surviving with health problems that led to early
deaths. Several local vets had been mortally scarred by
mustard gas. There was rejoicing when these veterans won
modest government pensions.

Before leaving home that morning we put a watermelon
in a washtub, on ice. Chicken was prepared the day before,
for chicken and dumplings. The meat, cut in pieces, lay
soaking in salt water. Mom believed that soaking removed

the blood, or the "wild" taste. Margie and I baked a cake, one of our favorites, from a flour bag recipe: a white cake made with lard, sugar, eggs, and maple flavoring, frosted half an inch thick and tinted bright red with food coloring.

Hens and Chicks

A hen was ready to set when she refused to leave the nesting box, ruffled her throat feathers, and glanced at you from the shadows with a suspicious red eye. Once off the nest, she clucked maternally, as though a parade of chicks followed her.

Three hens chose almost simultaneously to set, which meant a rush on our egg supply. Most fowl could accommodate up to a dozen eggs. For three weeks the setters sat, clucking softly as they turned eggs with their beaks. Turning guaranteed that the embryos would not adhere to the inside of the shells. Every two days we would close the henhouse door to the other birds and scatter grain. The setters emerged, exuded huge, noisome deposits of dung, ate and drank, and returned to their nests.

Of the forty-five eggs set to hatch, forty produced chicks. If a chick had trouble breaking through its shell, we assisted by enlarging the beak hole. By the end of spring, we hoped to have nearly two hundred chicks, which we would fatten, killing them in the fall, keeping only the sturdiest pullets for our new laying flock. My mother canned quarts of chicken for winter eating.

The chicks spent their first days on newspaper spread near the kitchen stove in an area blockaded by chunks of wood. An overturned cardboard box, with entry holes, supplied a hiding place. They ate cornmeal and oats. We each had favorites, which we gave names. Eventually, we divided them between the mothers. Brood hens avoided the main flock, preferring shade and concealment under low shrubs. No creatures are more brutal than hens. Helpless chicks are always in danger of being pecked to death. A hen bitten severely by deer flies is an easy victim of the flock. They peck at her head relentlessly until she dies. Runts are also the victims of this selective killing. We saved some hens by removing them in time and treating them with ointment. Curiously, Crip did not participate in these slaughters, leaving the dreary business to the hens.

Graduation

Five eighth-graders drove with Miss Crocker to the commencement exercises at Eagle River High School: Makinnen, Eileen Ewald, Bill Jolly, my cousin Grace, and I. Representing our school, I would present a three-minute speech. Miss Crocker worked on the text, a set of platitudes about the future, education, and the world as ours to win. I rehearsed it, assisted by Miss Crocker, a dozen times.

We had to wear suits. Mine was a new ugly brown plaid wool one that Dad had wangled from Welfare. The pants were incredibly baggy, rough, and cuffed.

The final week of school was a mixture of ebullience and sadness. Each afternoon we played games. Only the graduating students raised and lowered the flag. We also rang the hand bell. We agreed to divide the tadpoles, about thirty of them, we had nurtured in jars in the sandbox. All had legs and now resembled toads rather than frogs. I would keep mine until the tails were gone and then free them in a ditch. On the last day, we turned in our books and had lemonade and cookies. This was Miss Crocker's final year of teaching; she was marrying the town jeweler.

The commencement exercises were boring. Chairs had been set up on the stage. When the superintendent called the name of a school, the teacher and students took seats.

After the student representative spoke, diplomas were awarded, complete with handshakes and congratulations.

When my turn came, I arose, conscious of my ugly suit. I recited the first lines. Then someone laughed. Burning inside that wretched suit, I forgot my lines. With Miss Crocker's prompting, I was able to stumble on. I had let her down. Neither my mother nor my father attended — Dad couldn't leave work, and my mother felt she had no appropriate clothes. Her best dress was a gingham Welfare dress. This she was too proud to wear.

Fido

As a name for a dog "Fido" is neither clever nor original. It is a corruption of Fideles, or "Faithful" — a generic name evoking dog qualities.

Our Fido was short-haired and large, with orange and black markings. From the time he was a pup, he lived outdoors. Unless the weather turned impossibly cold, he remained in his doghouse, a structure built of old planking with a tar-paper roof and an entry hole just big enough for the dog to crawl through. We made the house small so that in bad weather his body heat would be contained to keep him from freezing. We never chained him.

He was a good watchdog. Given my fear of the woods and the dark, I took Fido with me whenever I walked in the forest or did night chores. He was fed almost entirely on table scraps — no canned or dried dog food. Occasionally he hunted, and we would find a chewed rabbit on the door stoop, or the remains of a wild duck. There were occasional mishaps with porcupines, and Dad would use a pliers to extract the needles from Fido's muzzle. When he was a year old, Dad castrated him with a razor blade, pouring on a mixture of oil cut with turpentine as a disinfectant. "Only way to keep him home," Dad said. After that, tamed, Fido lived out his life, finally falling victim to crippling arthritis contracted from those bone-chilling winters.

Miscarriage

Something was amiss that morning. Was it my mother's goiter acting up again? To avoid an operation, she'd answered an ad in a woman's magazine for an ointment and beads. The beads, amber seed shapes glued to small copper disks, were to absorb "vibrations" from the ointment, conducting "charges" to the swollen goiter tissue to dry it. For weeks she smeared her neck and wore the huckster's beads. When no lessening of the swelling occurred, she stopped using the beads.

She kept the beads in a shellacked tortoise shell on her dresser. I'd taken the shell from a mud turtle I caught in the strawberry patch. I boiled the turtle, and when the meat was soft I poked it loose with a stick and hung the shell in a tree until the remaining meat was eaten by ants. The shell rested on a piece of window glass near Mom's curling iron. The dresser's oval mirror was held in place by bent wood painted a mahogany tone, resembling horns. Nearby hung Mom's wedding picture. In exchange for three pullets, an itinerant photographer had enlarged a small photograph, the only one of the wedding extant, and framed it in a tin oval frame tinged rose and green.

I gave Mom hot coffee. She was facing the wall, utterly still.

"Mom?" She turned and smiled. "What is it?" I asked. She sat up and drank some coffee.

"I'll be all right," she said.

After a few moments I returned to the south pasture where I was helping Dad erect posts for a new pigpen. The spot was mud-luscious with dank, black soil. The pigs were ecstatic. When we finished, I returned to see how Mom was.

She had thrown off the quilts and was covered by a thin blood-stained sheet. "Get Dad," she said. "Hurry."

He came, gesturing for me to wait in the living room. Mom was weeping. Dad was consoling her and soon emerged with something wrapped in newspaper. "It was a new boy," he said, holding the wrapping to his side. He grabbed a shovel from the shed, went out behind the bedroom, and buried the baby near a small stand of white birch.

Mom was shivering. The bleeding would not stop. We piled quilts over her, and Dad went for the doctor.

The doctor we preferred, Oldfield, was out of town, so McMurray, the war ace, came. We were suspicious of him. My parents believed he was drunk when he delivered my brother and put too much silver nitrate in Everett's eyes. For weeks Everett had been blind.

The doctor finally emerged from the bedroom, saying that the baby had been five months along. He didn't want to see it. He gave my mother paregoric for the pain, and with flannel cloths stanched the blood, which he said would have stopped of its own accord "via the body's natural healing." He warned of complications and then patted my head. "You didn't need another brother anyhow, lad. Too many mouths to feed as it is."

This was Mom's third miscarriage; only one had been intentional. She had tried to miscarry Everett. Isolated and homesick for North Dakota, facing a difficult life after Margie and I were born, she had wanted no more babies. When she found herself pregnant with Everett, she sought advice from my uncle Pete's wife, Kate, the French Canadian who specialized in mild necromancies. She recommended ghastly mixtures of cod-liver oil, ground chicken gall bladders, strong coffee, moisture gathered from cows' udders, and honey, warmed into a smooth blend and swallowed neat. The child remained firmly *in utero*. Mom would load my sister and me into a wicker baby buggy and push it for hours over graveled roads, thinking she could jar the fetus loose. Nothing worked. She blamed herself for Everett's maladies, the bad eyesight, mild epilepsy, and slowness to learn.

Dad drove McMurray back to town, and Mom finally slept. Margie and Nell returned from Aunt Kate's, where Dad had sent them for the day. When I told Margie what had happened, she listened and then went to the kitchen and made herself a peanut butter sandwich. I sat down on the floor, holding Fido to my chest.

Timber

On weekends I accompanied Dad to Buckotaban Lake, where we peeled logs for the Wisconsin-Michigan Lumber Company. Dad and a friend, Marion Briggs, were hired to strip bark from the logs and pile them so that sledges and tractors could reach them for easy hauling. Briggs was a tall, husky man in his thirties, with a small daughter. He had been abandoned by his wife, reputedly a Spanish dancer. His mother raised the girl, keeping her in home-made dresses of an ugly Victorian style. Briggs was a violinist who, under mysterious circumstances, had given up his career. Only rarely would he consent to perform. He encouraged Dad to play instruments. They earned thirty cents for each log trimmed of branches and debarked. By working hard, they could finish six or seven trees an hour. My job was to peel logs Dad had trimmed and slashed along one side. I used a "spud," or tire iron. Pine bark came off easily. The spruce were difficult though. On these I used a drawknife, a blade with two parallel handles, scraping free the obstinate bark without gouging the wood. Since I was slow, Dad worked most of the spruce himself. The best logs would be sawed into lumber, the remainder pulped. Our clothes and hands were coated with pitch. Only kerosene would cut it.

Briggs worked by himself, creating his own piles of timber. One afternoon he walked over to me, chatted briefly, and then whipped out his penis. There's a protocol for relieving yourself in the presence of other males: either you turn your back or you stand beside them, facing the same way; neither of you gazes at the other. Briggs's member was almost equine; I had never seen anything like it. Dad came over and spoke curtly to Briggs, who never displayed himself to me again.

Ethics

Dad's trustworthiness and honor were tarnished by a feeling he shared with others of his subculture. Whenever you could exploit either the "haves" or the "government," you did it. One evening he invited me to go with him for a walk. After a quarter of a mile or so, we came to a rise of highland where the soil had been freshly shoveled. "There," he said proudly. "I've buried dynamite." He had stolen the explosives from his WPA job, intending to use them for excavating a basement. Over the basement he planned to build an extra room. He described the sensitivity of the caps, how a brusque hit would detonate them. The foreman made regular reports of the dynamite supply to superiors. If he came up short, they would investigate. Dad cautioned me to tell no one.

I carried this burden for weeks, forgetting the dynamite only when snow blew and the ground froze. Whether the rip-off ethic was generic to our class only, I do not know. Is one a thief if he takes from the rich? Later, when I worked in grocery stores, I took cakes, soft drinks, and packages of lunch meat and, hiding in the basement among stored boxes of food, had great feasts. These "fringe benefits," unofficially bestowed, would never be missed, I thought. So far as I knew, Dad never used the dynamite, nor was his cache discovered by the authorities.

Music

Dad gave me a Spanish guitar, one he had bought through a correspondence school. Dad played accordion, violin, and mandolin at taverns, usually accompanied by Charlie Mattek, who played guitar and sang. Dad said that if I practiced, I could join the duo and make some money.

Dad bought a guitar book, and with his usual patience, showed me how to place my fingers — G-F-G — and to strum time. Once I learned chords, he played his violin and I accompanied him. His favorite tunes were sentimental country songs from his childhood or ones he had learned as a roustabout and farm hand: "Over the Waves," "Red River Valley," "I'm Dreaming Tonight of Sweet Hallie," "The Prisoner's Song," "Red Wing." He made no effort to learn popular songs.

Hardly a day passed without his playing or singing. He sang us to sleep, holding both child and banjo on his lap. On the rare occasions when we had company, Dad performed. On good days we would take kitchen chairs to the front yard and play. The music seemed so perfect, so pure in contrast to our lives.

Although I learned to manipulate a handful of guitar chords, I never mastered the skill of picking out solos. I strummed mechanically, rarely feeling the music. When I later played tuba in the high school band, despite hours of practice, my playing was rote. I lacked Dad's spontaneity; he could relax, and, immersing himself wholly in his art, produce music.

Part Three: Summer

The Jollys

By traversing Ewald's forty and our own, we reached Perch Lake, the best of all nearby lakes for swimming. Minnow, nearer our house, was thick with bloodsuckers. And wading was impossible — you were soon up to your knees in muck. Perch Lake had a wide sandy shore and a sandy bottom. To get to the beach you had to cross a large potato field owned by a bad-tempered bachelor, John Simon, the town grave digger, whose house was invisible from the lake.

A grassy bluff with scrub Norway pines overlooked the beach. By getting a good run, you propelled yourself into the water. We had contests to see who could jump the farthest. For a swimsuit I wore old jeans cut off above the knees. My sisters had one-piece suits from Sears. Nell, only four, rarely went with us. My cousin Grace's breasts had already formed. George Jolly delighted in flashing his rear at Grace — "mooning," he called it.

I enjoyed going to Perch Lake with the Jollys. George was my age, Bill a year older. They lived at the opposite end of Sundsteen, a mile and a half past the school. I thought nothing of walking the distance to meet them, and since there were no telephones, there was no way of knowing whether they would be home or not. They came from a huge family of ten children. Bill and George loved fishing and often went to Columbus Lake.

The Jolly house was a two-storey affair covered with gray shingles. It had the usual spread of outbuildings — a barn with lofts for hay, a henhouse, a pigsty, and corrals for cows. The father and the oldest son worked for the Wisconsin-Michigan Lumber Company. Mrs. Jolly was an ebullient

woman with huge breasts who wore the same dress for
months, until it turned to shreds. All of her dresses were of
the same magenta Rit tint, the hue rubbed dull by grease
and child-soil.

The downstairs living room doubled as a bedroom. Here
the parents slept in a single bed with the three smallest
children. Upstairs, the four boys shared another bed, as
did the girls, Margaret, Helen, and Lucille. No rooms had
rugs or linoleum. Bill and George would lie on the floor
directly over the dining table, collect bed fluff, wood slivers,
and mouse turds, and drop them through a crack into a
pan of baked beans below. Daily, Mrs. Jolly baked bread
and cinnamon rolls. She gave me thick slabs of hot bread
smeared with bacon grease and peanut butter or wild-
cherry ("pincherry") jam. There was never enough silver-
ware. The family ate at a rectangular oak table in two shifts,
the older girls feeding the younger children. In the center
of the clothless table, near a platter of fried pike and perch,
stood the blue roaster full of beans. Bread, homemade jelly,
butter, lard, fresh milk, coffee. To help yourself to food you
simply reached into the roaster and then wiped your fingers on some bread. No plates matched, and most were
cracked. Only the parents used spoons and forks. Cinnamon rolls. Fresh gooseberry pie.

At school Bill and George often took my part against
Osmo Makinnen. Bill, blond, short, and muscular, was
quieter than George, who had black hair like mine and was
always mischievous. Both were good students. The three of
us would start high school together. Bill later died at Monte
Cassino in the early years of the war.

From the Jollys I learned how to fish, and they taught me
the little I knew about sex. They seemed wiser than I,
perhaps because they had older brothers, perhaps because
they were raised far more permissively; their mother
hardly had time to linger over their nurturing.

For our night swims in Perch Lake, Bill would bring
matches, and after we swam, we'd rustle up wood for a fire.

Bill had already reached manhood, but George and I lingered in late adolescence. One evening, George and I, naked, were horsing around, grabbing one another. Bill squatted near the fire watching. When George wrestled me to the sand, pinning my shoulders, Bill came over. His penis was hard. He started to play with it. George also began masturbating. I sat hunkered with my head on my knees, amazed, excited, yet vaguely embarrassed. Out in the lake, hundreds of toads swam toward our fire. As they hopped frantically ashore, we beat them with sticks and threw them into the flames. Then we doused the fire and left the beach.

Albert

My aunt Kate's eldest son, Albert, was illegitimate. His father, according to talk, was a handsome roustabout who had slept with Kate and then abandoned her before Albert was born. Dad always feared Kate. He blamed her for his brother Pete's death at age fifty-three, ostensibly from eating stale bologna sandwiches. Kate, Dad surmised, had tired of Pete, as she had of her other men. Dad feared he would be her next victim.

At twenty-one, Albert was a shy, lanky, sandy-haired youth with an engaging smile. He loved cars and had bought his own Model A from wages he earned at the local lumber mill. My uncle forced him to contribute most of his salary as room and board. To his mother and stepdad, he was a quasi-slave. He seemed to accept his persecutions; his mother never took his side, favoring the legitimate sons.

He often took me riding in his car, and I helped him with his chores. One evening, as we were playing five hundred rummy, a storm came up. My aunt said I should stay over. Albert offered to share his bed. During the night, he embraced me.

On the last Sunday of June, we went fishing for muskellunge. Albert's girlfriend, Rose Howe, came with us. We
rowed through connecting streams to a pair of lakes on the
famous Chain of Lakes, lakes ideal for muskie. Landing
muskellunge was difficult. Rich sportsmen carried revolv-
ers for the purpose, shooting the exhausted fish while it was
in the water.

I trolled my line, and Albert trolled his. We used chub
minnows for bait. At noon we ate lunch, had a swim, and
then turned the boat against the current, toward town. I
helped with the rowing. As we neared the channel, Albert
got a strike, a big one! To play the fish until it was
exhausted, we turned the boat around, facing the open
lake. Fifteen minutes later, Albert managed to play the
muskie close to the boat.

The fish was almost four feet long, a prizewinner.
Though subdued, he might suddenly flash forth, ripping
the hook from his mouth or even damaging the boat.
Albert threw a mesh bag over him and drew it tight against
the boat. While Rosa and I held the bag, Albert rammed a
gaff at the skull, piercing it. The stunned fish thrashed for
several minutes and then died.

My uncle, I was later told, dismissed the catch as paltry
and berated Albert for taking the day off without his
permission: He should have cultivated corn. His mother
refused to cook the fish, even after Albert cleaned it. He
gave most of the meat, wrapped neatly in newspaper, to my
dad, keeping a steak for himself. He shellacked the head,
mounted it on a pine board, and hung it near his bed.

The next morning he found the mounted head crushed
flat on its board. His brother Jim had smashed it with a
hammer. An altercation ensued. From the start, Albert had
the better of Jim—until their mother appeared and started
to beat Albert with a stick. Jim swung an axe at Albert, who
grabbed it and sent it flying into the grass. Jim retreated to
his room, locking himself in. Kate screamed, berating
Albert, claiming he had cut her. She seemed to want to

drive him to more violence, to the suicide he had threatened on more than one occasion.

Albert entered the house, grabbed a .22 rifle, and
declared he would kill himself. Near the road, a few feet
from his car, he died, a single clean hole visible behind his
ear.

Hysterical, Kate sent my cousin Frenchy for my dad —
Uncle Pete was in town. Albert appeared to be sleeping on
his side with his knees drawn up. The gun was still in his
hand, his finger on the trigger. The bullet hole seemed no
larger than a hornet's bite. My mother stayed with Kate,
who was screaming that it was all Albert's fault. Dad drove
to town for the sheriff and the undertaker.

The funeral, two days later, was at Gaffney's. A funda-
mentalist preacher said a few words, but nothing personal,
since he had seen Albert only twice in his life and my aunt
and uncle were not members of his flock.

Some deaths jolt survivors into something like enlighten-
ment over the cryptic and tragic nature of life. Albert's
death served that function. I stand now in memory at the
site, the luxuriant grass crushed where his body lay. I visit
his grave. There are no answers.

Garden and Field

The survival equation was clear: The harder we worked
during the brief growing season, about ninety days, the
better supplied with food we'd be for winter. Once the
potatoes blossomed and the corn grew silk, the soil
required mounding. When hilled, potatoes reproduced
more prolifically, and corn plants better withstood wind
and rain. Cheap canvas gloves protected our hands.
Against sunburn, we wore straw hats.

We hoed for entire mornings or afternoons, stopping
only long enough for swigs of ice-cold water from mason

jars. We took pride in our neat rows, knowing Dad would be pleased.

By early July, potato bugs appeared. For picking these one by one, Dad paid us a nickel a quart. The bugs spit orange juice and stank. We filled quart jars, which we dumped into a pail of kerosene to kill the bugs. We also examined the undersides of leaves for deposits of orange eggs. We either picked the infested leaves and crushed them or rubbed the sides of the leaf together into an orange mush.

The vegetable garden required more weeding and hoeing than the fields. Radishes matured first, followed by string beans and peas. We picked the ripe vegetables and helped my mother can them. Beets—not one of our favorites—and carrots matured late. These we buried in sand under the living room floor. When the sweet corn was ready, we ate it at numerous meals and spent hours shucking and slicing kernels for canning. Dad made a special rack for the jars so we could process a whole wash boiler at a time. By September, the cellar shelves were crammed with jars. The cobs we fed to the pigs.

Of all the crops, strawberries and rhubarb were the most resistant to insects and diseases. We always had luck with strawberries, and we devoured gigantic shortcakes topped with mounds of whipped cream.

Rumors of War

We took no daily newspaper and no magazines, and we rarely listened to radio news. The Sunday paper, which we bought, was long on features and short on current events. The editors loved sex murders, Edward VIII and Mrs. Simpson, and Indian children raised by wolves.

In 1936 Hitler occupied the Rhineland. Italy annexed Ethiopia. King George V died and was succeeded by

Edward VIII, who soon abdicated for Mrs. Simpson. The
Spanish Civil War started, as did the war between China
and Japan. Dachau was in operation. *Life* magazine first
appeared in November 1936; we received a notice in the
mail and subscribed. European turmoils rarely figured in
its pages. Hitler was seldom mentioned. Parties, rich foods,
new kitchen gadgets, and arcane moments in popular culture were featured. Nothing was designed to produce a
single tremor of dismay in American readers, nor to
inform them of the impending war.

Dad's friend, George Botteron, on a visit with his family
insisted we tune the radio to Father Coughlin, the Jew-
baiting, Hitler-loving Roman Catholic priest. Coughlin
opened broadcasts with Hitler addressing the masses.
When Dad expressed disgust, the Botterons stopped their
visits.

Dad did, however, share the local distaste for Jews from
Milwaukee and Chicago who made up our summer tourist
population. To the impoverished locals, they were osten-
tatious with money, cars, and clothes. The women's makeup
and scanty shorts were considered offensive. Their "pushi-
ness" was also legend: they would shove you off the side-
walk, we believed. Caddies joked about serving Jewish
women. They let the shorts-wearing players tee their own
balls, so the caddies could catch glimpses of intimate flesh.
The anti-Semitic myth of Jews as nontippers persisted.
When Jewish golfers needed caddies, we often tried to hide
behind the caddie shack.

Jews were shamelessly excluded from all resorts except
one. Not until 1948, after World War II, were signs
announcing "Restricted Clientele" prohibited by law. The
single resort catering to Jews was Eagle Waters. Any locals
working there as handymen or maids were regarded as
inferior by those employed at gentile resorts. Fishermen
kept their boats well back from the river fronting Eagle
Waters, certain that Jewish sewage contaminated the game
fish.

Many girls were more than willing victims, falling for
promises of a glamorous, rich life away from Eagle River.
Most such promises were summer-short. When the
Lotharios returned to the city, the girls remained behind
disillusioned, tainted, and often with child, accusing the
summer residents of having shamelessly exploited them.
No hard-working local male would marry such used goods.
The conflict between the local ethos of poverty, constancy,
and illiteracy and the glamorous allure of city life destroyed
many of these girls and intensified the anti-Semitism. Some
girls lingered in the town. Once their beauty faded, they
turned to alcohol, welfare, and prostitution. Others disappeared into the cities to the south.

One Jew, Harry Holperin, lived permanently in Eagle
River. He reputedly had sold apples on the streets of
Chicago during the Depression, eventually earning
enough money to buy a grocery in Eagle River. Here he
married a gentile and became a town booster. His grocery
carried foods for the tourist trade. He was accepted as a
"white Jew," which meant he was inconspicuous and not
pushy. When he grew rich, he still lived in modest rooms
above his store. He traveled often to Milwaukee, where it
was rumored he had complex business dealings. His wife,
Orpha, helped by his two sons, looked after the grocery.
Since the store was seasonal, after Labor Day it opened only
on weekends. Holperin, a gracious man of much charm,
contributed generously to the high school band fund, and
he gave numerous local boys their first jobs, training them
in his store. I was one of these boys, and remain most
grateful to him and to his family.

Anti-Semitism was thoroughgoing, worsening during
the summer when tourists tripled the population. Since
they constituted no economic threat, Indians were less the
butt of prejudice. Dislike for Indians festered month after
month, but anti-Semitism was far more virulent. No blacks
were visible in town, either as inhabitants or tourists. After
World War II, as locals migrated to work in the auto plants

of Racine, Milwaukee, and Beloit and competed with blacks for menial jobs, more bigotries arose. Most locals cheered Hitler's efforts to control the Jews; however, most, I think, would have been horrified by the gas chambers.

Fourth of July

The Fourth of July was a replay of Memorial Day, without the funereal solemnities. Dr. McMurray's services were not required — no commemorative wreaths were dropped from his biplane to honor dead servicemen. The July parade was more elaborate and stressed humor. Clowns sought to keep an old Model T running. Floats carried bathing beauties tossing candy, Indians in regalia, local politicians, mounted cowboys dressed like Gene Autry. Other floats urged more fishing, hunting, and golf. The parade disbanded at the county fairgrounds where in the evening there would be fireworks.

At home we feasted on chicken and dumplings, fresh lettuce drenched with milk and sugar, tomatoes, pies, and watermelon. The day was sultry, continuing the pattern for the week. Despite our high elevation, over a thousand feet, our usually dry air was uncomfortably humid. Huge mosquitoes swarmed. Unless you had immunity, venturing into the woods and swamps was a nightmare of mosquito attacks. We sprayed the cattle twice a day. Not only were they plagued by mosquitoes, but huge flies burrowed through their hides, depositing eggs in clusters beneath the skin. The spray, bought from a Watkins dealer, did not kill insects but was sufficiently noisome to keep them from alighting. If we failed to protect Lady, her milk dried up.

We managed to keep the house fairly free of mosquitoes. Screens fit well, and my mother nagged us to keep the doors closed. Evenings, we took a pail with holes punctured in the sides, arranged dry wood shavings in the bottom, lighted them, added more wood, and then covered the fire with green grass. We burned this smudge throughout the house. The thick smoke either drove the insects out or numbed them so we could smash them.

On warm evenings we sat in the front yard, with the smudge drifting over, protecting us. We believed that, once bitten, if you allowed the mosquito to fill himself with blood, withdraw, and fly off, it would not leave an itching welt. We also thought that a blood-logged mosquito would soon die. Citronella helped minimize their bites. Since the lotion was expensive, we used it sparingly, primarily when we were in the woods or fields.

Tornado

Nell saw the first indigo clouds swelling to the east. "That's a bad one," Dad said. "It's over at Minocqua and speeding this way." The stilled air had gotten several degrees colder. We pulled in the chairs from the front yard. Everett took the cow and calf to the barn. A vast current, like a great river, whirled through the upper sky, crackling and snapping. Near the ground, all was frighteningly calm. The storm clouds, still some distance off, resembled great churning brains, the deep blacks and indigos slashed with lightning. Then, horrified, we realized that a funnel was heading for us! Its swirling tail was light-colored, almost white, in contrast with its body. It whipped treetops in its path.

Dad said we'd be safest on the floor, where we could scoot under the table. The thunder was horrendous. Birch trees swept the ground. Sheets of rain scudded past the window. The house shuddered. Guy wires holding the stovepipe to the roof snapped and flapped. The lightning was incessant. Everything was pitch black. A pair of birds flung themselves against the window. We found them later, dead.

The storm passed. The sun came out, producing a beautiful rainbow.

We checked the animals and found the barns and coop intact. The tornado had cut a huge swath through the woods, barely missing Kula's farm. We drove to town to see the damage. Except for the loss of a few roofs, Eagle River was spared. Near Conover the storm had uprooted trees for a mile. The violence was incredible. It would take years for the forest to return.

Church

I continued to attend the Lutheran Church, was baptized, and two weeks after Easter had my parents, sisters, and brother baptized. I hurried through catechism in order to teach Sunday school, a class of fourth-graders. I was soon promoted to superintendent. My duties were simple: call the sessions to order, lead prayers, conduct the offering of pennies, teach my class, conclude the session with another prayer, count and record the offering, and then attend the adult services in the nave.

Each Saturday night, just before going to sleep, I worked over my Sunday lesson. The church provided booklets, each featuring a colored picture illustrating the biblical text to be studied. Teachers received simple teaching manuals and were encouraged to memorize a psalm each Sunday, our students one per month. I affixed gold crosses to study papers whenever a student completed a psalm. I rarely missed memorizing, reciting both on my walk in to church and on the return home. My pedagogical methods derived from the belief that passionate prayer resolved all problems. It seemed to work, even with a pair of smart alecks whose dads were church trustees. Although my mother rarely attended services, Dad usually drove us to Sunday school. I preferred to walk whenever I could, memorizing psalms.

Eventually, Dad got himself a blue serge Welfare suit, attended church, and made a friend of Rev. Krubsack, who would come to the house on visits. The reverend liked laborers, probably because of his own working-class German origins. His lugubrious air of learning, however, prevented his ever being "one of us." His sermons, delivered in rich guttural tones, were often scary. Among his principal tenets were the following: 1. Simply by being born, you have broken all ten commandments. 2. Since the only way to Eternal Life is through Jesus' intercession, and since He finds public confessions of sin distasteful, the best way to catch His ear is to pray solo, in your closet with the door closed. 3. All church organizations except the Ladies' Aid are suspect and disallowed. 4. Roman Catholics are anathema. 5. No good Lutheran boy or girl will join the Scouts—they put too much emphasis on doing good deeds and not enough on asking Christ's forgiveness for your having broken His commandments. 6. A communicant must register at least a day in advance of taking Communion, as a guarantee that the parishioner will not "drink damnation unto himself."

It was difficult to admire someone so rigid, but I tried to live his ideals. Later, when I was drafted into the army, for nearly two years, I wrote him for permission to take Communion from a cleric not of the Missouri Synod faith. When, of necessity, I ate the wafer and drank the wine without first securing Krubsack's approval, I felt as much grace without his permission as with it. From that experience dates my fall from organized religion.

Learning to Drive the Car

My propensities for flinching delayed my learning to drive. Dad, incredibly patient, seated beside me in the Model A, would guide me through the gears. My Achilles' heel was sensing the exact moment for releasing the clutch.

One Sunday Dad stopped the car in the middle of Sundsteen Road. "You drive," he said, just like that.

He turned off the engine and changed seats. I set the choke and started the ignition. He cautioned me to release the clutch slowly. I tensed, pushed in the clutch, set the gear, and released the clutch. There was a loud rumble and clank. I had broken the axle! Why couldn't I learn something so simple? Other boys did. "Next time you'll get it," Dad said. We pushed the car off the road. "Well, let's get Kula."

Kula returned with his horses and pulled us home. Dad was greatly inconvenienced—for a week he had to walk a good mile to catch a ride to work. He traded a pig for a new axle, brought it home, and on the next weekend repaired the Ford.

He insisted I try again; delaying would only make it harder to learn. This time we practiced near home. Caution paid off. I learned to feel that subtle moment when the clutch releases itself and the car moves forward. Within days I was driving short distances up and down the road.

Eventually, I bought myself a used Model A, and learned to make minimal repairs. If I had patience, it appeared, I had mechanical aptitude. I learned also that smearing your hands with grease and grit was not an odious experience.

Dad never teased me about my differences from other boys. My brother, for instance, loved cars and hunting. Dad encouraged my "book" education, saying he hoped I wouldn't end up digging ditches as he had to. He helped me buy an old reconditioned Underwood typewriter through the Sears, Roebuck catalogue.

Columbus Lake

I met Bill and George Jolly one morning at their house at 6 A.M. Their seventeen-year-old brother, John, a freckled, husky youth, was still asleep on the bed the three of them shared. He was lying on his back and his sheet had worked up across his chest, revealing a sizable erection. George settled a noose of fishing line around John's penis and dropped the loose end of the line out a nearby window. "Watch," he laughed, running downstairs.

The black thread moved with delicate tugs. John grew even more erect. George yanked harder, and John awoke, cursing. "That's George doin' it again, right?" Keeping the string taut, he went over to the window and urinated. George yelled, ran back upstairs, and proceeded to wrestle his naked brother to the floor.

Later, while George ate breakfast, I helped Bill dig night crawlers. They loaned me a cane pole; they each had casting rods. They jammed some bread and cheese into a bag, which would serve also for bringing fish home.

To reach the lake we traversed a superb stand of virgin timber—pine, hemlock, and cedar, with some yellow birch. Partridge flew from thickets. When we reached a floating bog, I matched my footprints to George's. One misstep and you were up to your waist in muck. As it was, on any portion of the bog your feet were under water. The trick was to leap to the next clump before the mass sank deeper under your weight. The vast lake was visible a hundred yards off. We soon reached high land and a rapid creek that flowed into the lake.

We dropped our gear on the sand and stripped to our underwear. The shallow water was rife with pickerel weed. Beyond was a drop-off where Bill planned to fish. We tied fish stringers and a small bag of worms around our waists. George showed me how to bait the hook.

Bill hooked two walleyes and some bass and bluegills. George caught a pickerel, which he threw back, saying it was too bony, and nearly a dozen bass, bluegills, and large perch. My catch consisted of six bluegills and three smallmouth bass.

We stopped for lunch, stripped, and had fun swimming and splashing. When we were thirsty, we simply scooped up handfuls of water and drank. A doe and a fawn appeared. A black bear, fortunately without cubs, spied us and waddled back into the forest. While Bill continued fishing, George and I lay stretched out on the sand, absorbing sun and talking about girls. He claimed that he "did it" with Alice Carlson. She was the oldest of a brood of children left motherless when their mother had died giving birth. I knew George was fibbing, yet I chose to believe him, enhancing his prowess, fearsome and mysterious to me. Perhaps I had a crush on George, of the kind youths have on one another. I don't know. The more masculine—and crude—he was, the better I liked him. I wished for the afternoon never to end.

Impregnation

Charlie Mattek had staked his Guernsey bull in the north pasture, waiting for Lady. When I led her to the gate, the huge Guernsey caught her scent, grew aroused, reached the end of his tether, and pawed the ground. While he grew frenetic, his penis dripping, Lady seemed oblivious of him and kept munching grass, well beyond his reach. When Charlie pulled Lady nearer, the bull began licking her, his penis a hot rod of meat ready for penetration. He shuddered and withdrew, lowing. Strings of semen dripped from Lady. "That should do it," Charlie said. I led Lady home. I was to bring her back if she remained in estrus.

The Botterons

Visits from local families were rare. Only the Botterons spent occasional Sunday afternoons with us, until the quarrel over Father Coughlin. When he was in his teens, George

Botteron immigrated from Glarus, Switzerland, and married a Polish woman from Chicago. Rose babbled as much in Polish as she did in English, which often disconcerted my mother. There were three children: Norman, Rose Helen, and Gerald. Norman, the oldest, was my age. We lived too far away for walking, so roughly once a month we exchanged visits by car.

The Botterons taught me off-color Polish words. The only one I remember is *pitchkie,* for penny-bank slit, or vagina. There were a few insults and curses, mostly based on the reputed stupidity of Slavs. Norman arranged "shows" with his sister and a neighbor girl. For a penny each, the girls would pee in coffee cans.

George Botteron was an accordionist, so he and Dad played music. Rose Botteron's hatred of Jews was utterly irrational and derived from her girlhood in a Chicago slum. She seemed the archetypal farm wife, tending to animals and fowl, her apron filled with grain or fat brown eggs. Norman, Gerald, Everett, and I fashioned slingshots and arrows for hunting birds — we never bagged any — and played endless games of tag and giant step.

One afternoon the Botteron kids and I returned from swimming in Perch Lake. Norman, in a loud bragging voice, tattled to the adults that I had pulled up some of old John Simon's potatoes. True, I had been thoughtless, showing off; I had merely wanted to see how big the potatoes were. Norman had promised not to tell.

Botteron dared Dad to punish me. When I blurted out that it was only *one* hill, Dad yanked me to him, turned me over his lap, and spanked me. He threatened to tell the sheriff next day when he went to work.

I hid in the grove behind the house, staying until after dark. The fact that my punishment had occurred in front of visitors hurt far worse than the spanking itself. Why did Dad need to save face? Before that he had never once slapped me.

For a week I spent most of each day hidden in the woods, positive that the sheriff would haul me to jail. I hid close to the house to be ready to run if an officer drove up. I feared asking Dad if he had indeed notified the sheriff. He had no inkling of the effect of his discipline on me.

Caddying

A few hours of training prepared you for the Eagle Waters Golf Course, a nine-hole course that covered a picturesque area of pine and birch groves winding near a major channel that connected the vast series of lakes known as the Chain of Lakes. Here, muskellunge fishing was the best in the world. To reach the club we hitchhiked fifteen miles to the Chanticleer Inn. From their boat dock we shouted across to the clubhouse, where the caddy master, doubling as bartender, sent a boat to fetch us.

An experienced caddy walked us through a few holes, showing us how to hold the pin-flag to keep it from flapping and deflecting the player's concentration. We were advised to walk a few steps behind our player, always to the left, ready to supply any club he wished. We were to keep our mouths shut unless spoken to — "and keep your eye on the ball." Our first responsibility was to know where a ball flew and to lead the player to it. Seventy-five cents for nine holes. The caddy master, Jack Bacich, was impressed whenever players asked for us a second time. We contributed our tips to a kitty, divvied up by Bacich or his sister Betty at the end of each week. As I recall, the Bacichs took 15 percent for "managing" the fund. They kept complaints to a minimum by giving us free ice cream bars or Frozen Turkey candy, a white nougat marshmallow treat. Some days we sat around for hours, waiting to work. We talked dirty a lot. Occasionally there was the titillation of pocket-sized obscene treatments of "Maggie and Jiggs," "Out Our Way,"

"Blondie," and "The Katzenjammer Kids," circulated by the older caddies who had purchased them at a local gas station. Moon Mullins pumped Maggie; his organ was as fat as his forearm.

A high point was the Homeowners' Loan Corporation Golf Tournament, sponsored by the Chanticleer Inn, with prizes going to the winners and their caddies. Bacich assigned us to players according to our seniority. Most caddies worked the week, earning $25 before tips. We usually served the same player, unless he complained to the caddy master, who then switched us around. One player I held in particular awe was Edgar Guest, the most popular poet of the day. He was a short, pudgy man who wore plaid knicker-type golf pants and a plaid cap with a visor. His verses, widely syndicated in newspapers, reached a huge audience. His most famous lines were "It takes a heap o' livin' / to make a house a home." He stood for easy values and the virtues of everyday lives. Another of his much-loved poems was an ode to the outhouse, that structure so indigenous to rural America.

Whenever I wrote poems, I wrote in his manner. At six I had attempted verses and short stories based on cute animals — raccoons, possums, skunks, frogs, crows, and robin redbreasts. My first public recognition came when the superintendent of schools saw one of my Rocky Raccoon stories, written in a pencil tablet. When the teacher singled me out, the superintendent patted my head and told me to keep writing. That spring I wrote poems, hoping to enter one in the county fair. Miss Crocker selected a narrative piece and drew a picture to go with it. That fall I realized she had written an entirely new poem, "The Teacher with a Bully in His Class," and entered it in my name. She had printed it in Gothic script and affixed a drawing of an old-fashioned schoolmaster berating a hulking, obstreperous boy standing by, waiting to be birched. The poem received first prize, a new dollar bill. When I questioned the ethics—

the work after all, was hers — Miss Crocker laughed and said that I had tried so hard to write she wanted to "assist" me. After that, I kept my verses private, limiting myself to an occasional story and keeping elaborate notes on meetings of our "literary club." Among the few books constituting our school library was Guest's famous volume *The House by the Side of the Road.*

I took every opportunity to watch Guest tee up and drive his ball down the fairway. He was an indifferent golfer, but because of his fame he was assigned our most experienced caddy, Mike Tomlanovich. On Friday, the last day of the tournament, I screwed up my courage and asked him to autograph a golf card, which I then prized for years. The paradox of a True Poet (as I regarded him then) arranging home mortgages, a form of usury, never struck me. He certainly was a departure from my naive image of the poet as a romantic loner in lace cuffs, seated at an open casement window at dusk, plume in hand, seized by Inspiration.

The golf course was my first real involvement with the world outside home and school. This, a real job, differed from selling arbutus, peeling logs, and picking potato bugs — jobs I had done for my dad. For the first time, I sensed real possibilities in the larger world.

Finn Hall

A closed community of Finns inhabited Phelps, a lumber town north of Eagle River. Importing cooperative ideals from Europe, these people found a locale of hills, firs, lakes, and swamps resembling the homeland. They established a cooperative sawmill, grocery and hardware stores, a school, a health service, and a cow fund. If any of their group lost cows from disease, calving, or drowning, the fund replaced the animal. They believed in free and uni-

versal education from grade school through university.
Their ideals, like those of other immigrant Scandinavians
settling in Wisconsin and Minnesota, influenced the culture
at large. The Progressive party, led by Senator Bob La Fol-
lette of Wisconsin, set a national tone that incorporated
Scandinavian social values.

A conspicuous Finnish effort at community outreach was
the erection of a hall for meetings, festivals, and dances.
These events supported the cow and family funds. The
hall, built of pine logs, was located a half mile from Sundsteen School. Across the road was a grove of virgin ever-
greens, a spot I always feared. The deep recesses might
easily conceal bear or a leech-covered wild man of the
woods. One winter morning I found blood all over the
snow and decided a man had been killed there. My quieter
mind said that it was a deer. A fetid odor of death emerged
from the sunless earth below the gigantic cedars.

The Finnish overseers scheduled Saturday night dances,
charging half a dollar for each male attending. They
imported a trio of semiprofessional musicians from
Watersmeet, Michigan, who played both traditional and
popular music. My cousin Frenchy attended every dance,
drank, and got into fights. To many young men, the pursuit of violence was more important than the pursuit of
women.

No other place in the immediate area so appealed to
young bucks for acting out mating rituals, turf defenses,
and ego pecking orders. To my cousin, cut lips and black
eyes were badges of honor. Occasionally, Everett and I
walked to the hall to listen to the music. Once, in the
parking lot, we witnessed a vicious fight between Frenchy
and another husky youth. The excitement was palpable.
When Frenchy was getting the worst of it, his brother Jim
jumped in. Shortly, the fight turned into a melee. Officials
tried to stop it but couldn't. My brother and I, fearful, left
before the fight ended. The next day Frenchy and Jim
boasted they had smeared the gravel with their attackers,

men from Michigan looking for trouble. When the hall was finally closed to dances, the young stags moved to other venues to work their macho imperatives.

Wild Berries

Picking blueberries was a way of life. Families with knowledge of fertile patches were secretive. Farmers were alert to trespassers and threatened pickers found on their land. Berries were particularly lavish on burned-over state land near Buckotoban, twenty miles north. Such first crops on burned land were always prolific.

On the last Saturday of July, we packed bologna sandwiches, lemonade, cookies, and coffee, threw a galvanized washtub and an assortment of lard pails into the car, and drove to Buckotoban. When we arrived, cars were already parked, the pickers getting an early start. Dad drove down the circuitous dirt road until he came to a depression as large as a lake. Tall dead firs, still blackened from fire, stood at intervals. On the far bank, large hazelnuts flourished. We could find shelter there from the sun. A narrow stream we could drink from ran through the blueberry patch.

The shrubs were loaded, and there were huckleberries, darker than the blueberries and larger. Dad took his pail and went off alone, leaving the rest of us to stay within sight of the car. We tied pails to our waists with rope. Nell and Everett quickly tired and spent most of their time eating all they picked or napping. Mom was a fast picker, as I was. We were proud of how clean our berries were, with minimal leaf and twig chaff.

I worried when Dad was out of sight. What if he were lost? What if a grizzly loomed over us?

The most fecund shrubs flourished around the trunks of burned trees. The berries were so thick you simply cupped a branch with your hand, palm up, and raked your fingers through. Once a pail bottom was covered, filling the pail seemed easy. Each pail dumped into the washtub was another guarantee against winter's hunger.

By 5 P.M. we were within inches of filling the tub. We had picked nearly half the patch. Since we had concentrated near the road, Dad felt we'd find berries there next week. Cars looking for productive spots would stop, see the stripped bushes, and drive on. We reached home tired, ate cold chicken and tinned beef, and went to bed.

In the morning we cleaned the berries by passing them from one hand to the other, and blowing on them to dislodge light debris and withered fruit. In the steam processing, all green fruit would soften and absorb color. Once we'd filled a kettle, we floated the berries in water to wash off dust, scooping out any defective fruit. We filled sterilized quart jars and processed them in our wash boiler. By evening we had canned over fifty quarts.

The following Saturday we returned to Buckotoban, an outing as successful as the earlier one. After that we limited our picking to patches near the farm. One fertile spot was a bog on Kula's land. We had to be quiet there, for Kula, pitchfork in hand, chased trespassers. We ate this fruit raw in milk and sugar or cooked in thick pies smothered with homemade ice cream.

We also harvested raspberries, wild pincherries (for a delicious jelly), and blackberries. Raspberries grew on old brush heaps or stone piles. Garter snakes darted from hiding. We killed every snake we could, not realizing they were harmless and, in fact, controlled vermin. We whacked snakes in half with hoes or sticks, watching the halves squirm. We draped dead snakes on barbed-wire fences, a warning, we thought, to other snakes. I recall digging up a writhing nest, shoving the snakes into a tin can, clamping on a cover, and presenting them as a "present" to Margie. She closed her eyes and then opened them to find her hands filled with the writhing creatures. She ran screaming to the house.

None of us cared much for blackberries, although they made a superb jam. For several years, juneberries flourished. Then, suddenly, mysteriously, there were no more juneberries. All of the trees were dead.

Part Four: Fall

First Frost

The first week of September brought the first hard frost. Maple tree sap ebbed along myriad capillary streams, finally reaching the roots, where it remained all winter. It was the sap withdrawing that stained leaves with the persimmon, scarlet, and saffron tints that made those autumnal forests wondrous. Nights grew short, and the icily resplendent tones of aurora borealis formations covered the skies. In elaborate, noisy patterns, wild geese migrated south. Eagerly awaited parcels of school clothes arrived from Sears, Roebuck. My various summer jobs — caddying, stripping timber, selling arbutus, picking potato bugs — paid for the new clothes, with fifteen dollars left over. I had helped my family. I looked forward to the county fair, where we would exhibit livestock and produce, and the carnival preceding it. The cataclysms that continued to swirl through Europe seemed unreal. Our political sentiments were staunchly "America First."

Carnival

The carnival took place in a field at the junction of Sundsteen Road and Highway 17. I walked there before opening day to help erect tents and booths. Brightly painted vans were arranged in a row at the back of the field. Barred wagons, badly in need of paint, held a lion and a gorilla. Some booths were already up. There would be a ferris wheel and a merry-go-round. The carnies looked rough, most of them unshaven, some stripped to the waist. The women among them dressed like men.

A large tent was splayed over the dirt, ready for hoisting. Half a dozen men were driving stakes into the ground and tying guy ropes. "Don't just stand there!" a voice shouted. "Get to work." The man, in his mid-twenties, wore red trunks and was tanned a savage brown. His biceps were huge and flexed as he stood before me. His accent was strange. "He'p get this tent up and you'll earn a silver dollar."

I held the guy wires taut while he secured them to stakes. The crew raised the tent, working a large center pole upright. We erected shorter poles. The pungent odor of crushed grass blended with the snake-like smell of canvas.

We set up platforms for a trapeze and surrounded an area of painted boxes and hoops with a circle of wire, where the lion and gorilla would perform. Near the center pole stood an ornate calliope, which received power from a noisy generator.

When we broke for lunch, the carnival man invited me to his wagon. His name was Brik. He was from Georgia, and traveled with the show for half the year, moving north during the warm season and moving south when it got cold. He bossed the crew.

The interior of his wagon was set up like a living room, complete with small sofa and an embroidered, brightly colored pillow saying "I LUV U MOM." A small dinette contained a couple of chairs and an icebox, and a mattress and blankets were on the floor. "Like liverwurst?" he asked. "Sure," I said, sitting at the table. He brought out milk and pop. "Milk keeps my muscles big," he said. "I suppose you noticed."

"I want to look like you," I said, feeling stupid as soon as my words were out.

"You've got height, lad. Here, stand with your back against mine. You'll see."

His buttocks flared against mine. He tightened the muscles of his back.

"I was right. You're taller." He faced me. His chest was covered with curly black hair. "You'll have hair, and it'll be as black as mine." He laughed. "And you'll get muscles." He had grown up on a farm. "I like ramblin'," he said. "I could never be like my dad, married to some woman, with kids tying me down."

He smeared liverwurst on slabs of soft A & P white bread, piling the sandwiches on a paper plate. "Two's plenty," I said. His bare knees touched mine. He spread his legs. I felt giddy, swallowed milk, and finished my sandwich. A magnetic current from his knee jolted me. There was sweat on my lip.

"Well, let's get on. There's more work to do." If I stayed, in addition to the silver dollar, he'd see that I got a pass for the big tent show. "I wish you was older," he said. "I'd ask you to join this here carnival, and live with me."

Later, I went to his wagon to collect my pay and found him on his couch stark naked. "Don't get upset, lad. You've seen a man naked before. I have to wear my 'public duds' for tonight." I stole a look at his penis. It had an enormous foreskin. He pulled some dress pants on, felt in his pockets, and withdrew a silver dollar. "Don't see many of these around," he said. "Plenty in Colorado, though." He gave me a piece of paper saying "Tent Show: Admit One."

I thanked him. He told me that if I helped tear down the tents the next night, I'd earn another dollar.

All the way home, I heard his accent. In a trance, I milked the cow. I'd go anywhere he wanted, do anything he asked.

I plastered my hair with brilliantine. I regaled Margie with descriptions of the tiger (in actuality a defanged beast) and the gorilla. She would use my show pass; I'd sneak under the tent.

The Big Show was exciting, particularly the aerialists, billed as The Flying Godeckes From Poland. Spangles barely concealed the runs and tears in their tights. Glimpses of peach-colored flesh glowed whenever the woman balanced on her head and spread her legs and the trapeze turned.

The aerialist doubled as lion-tamer, while his partner put the gorilla through hoops and loops. A scrawny elephant, tuskless, performed listlessly with a girl dressed as a ballerina with glittering tiara sitting on his head. A pair of clowns pretended to throw pails of water at the audience; the water was feathers. During the show, Brik circulated, supervising the erection and removal of props.

I treated Margie to cotton candy and a sideshow featuring a fat woman with a second head growing from her side, a midget missing all fingers except for his thumbs, and a mummy, reputedly the body of John Wilkes Booth, stolen from its grave. Most fascinating of all was a lady geek. Once a night, so the hype went, she required a feast of hen's blood, Black Orpington, to be precise. We paid our fifteen cents and crowded close. A nervous hen was tied by its leg to a stake in the ground. Harsh recorded music, in scratchy violins, heralded I-Zelda's appearance. She undulated forth, painted like a gypsy and dressed in a gaudy skirt and layers of beads. "A good fat hen holds one pint of hot blood," a tout exclaimed. "For your admission you will observe I-Zelda, Princess of Turkey, bite this here black hen's throat. It will cost you another fifteen cents to see her suck out the life, killing the chicken dead!" He motioned us closer. "Anybody with a bad heart, leave now. What you are about to witness ain't for the squeamish!" No one left. Margie looked puzzled, then horrified.

With ceremonial gestures, I-Zelda smoothed her hands over her body, jangled her bracelets in a brief dance, circled the hen (now positioned between two large lighted candles), took up the fowl, and began sucking its beak. She pulled a scarlet scarf from her cincture and wound it about the hen, securing its wings. Taking the bird firmly by its feet, she placed its entire head in her mouth. The bird struggled. I-Zelda withdrew the head. Trickles of blood were visible on its throat. I-Zelda's mouth was bloody.

Margie was sick. We pushed our way through the crowd and started home. This incomplete act, like so many in a lifetime, assumed a mystical force. Was she a sorceress, or merely another desperate human performing an out-rageous act of survival?

I did not return to Brik the next evening. I stayed in the field all afternoon gathering and husking corn. I chopped wood. After supper, I lay in bed praying for Christ to quiet my turbulence. He approached with palms extended, the wounds visible. He smiled, His robes wafted by an aromatic breeze. As He neared, I saw that His face was the carnival man's!

County Fair

The fair was the social event of the year, and people you seldom saw surfaced. Clubs and lodges sold beer and food. Most families attended the entire three days. Livestock had to be fed, watered, and kept clean, so boys brought blankets and slept in the straw near their animals.

On Friday morning we loaded our sow and piglets and a dozen hens into a trailer. At the fairgrounds we secured pens and cages and attached entry tags; then we returned for garden produce and canned food—string beans and peas, pints of blueberry and strawberry jams, and a straw-berry-rhubarb pie.

By Saturday noon the judging was complete. My mother won firsts for jam and pie, seconds and thirds for the other entries. A plate of cucumbers, ears of sweet corn, and string beans also took firsts. The sow and piglets received a third, with a note scribbled by the judge saying that he doubted they were purebred. Our "white leghorn" pullets earned seconds. Here we fooled the judges: Before display-

ing the birds, we plucked black feathers, betraying their
impure breed, from their bodies. Our Plymouth Rock hen
took third, after a string of firsts the five preceding years.
Our winnings totaled $45.

A drunken, henna-haired Chicago lady was so enamored
of our piglets she suddenly reached into the pen and
grabbed one. As the animal wriggled and squealed, the
lady gave it a juicy, alcoholic kiss on the snout. The irate sow
narrowly missed the woman's arm.

To walk through the fairgrounds at night was to walk
through jewels: the lights ablaze, the smell of gasoline and
oil propelling the clanging ride motors, the hawkers
shouting from their booths, the melancholy music from the
merry-go-round pipe organ, the odors of animals and
flattened grass. How magical fairs were, so bizarre, so free.
The drifters who manned the rides and the skill booths,
and the scantily clad women who performed bumps and
grinds on the midway were truly glamorous!

At the very top of the ferris wheel I sat suspended by
fragile cable and thin steel, in a swinging wooden seat. The
starry sky seemed touchable, and the people below, walking
in the haze, were small dolls. When I saw my parents
strolling, holding hands, with my sister Nell following, I
was overwhelmed with love. Later I saw Dad pound at a
target with a sledgehammer, the bell he struck ringing
magically through the sky.

For the first time, I would appear in public with Dad and
Charlie Mattek, playing a medley of Dad's favorite accordion tunes. We were scheduled for Saturday night, as part
of the grandstand entertainment. Our fifteen-minute performance would follow a popular local singer, Helen
Byington, who imitated the renowned country singer Patsy
Montana. Our rehearsal times were limited to the preceding weekend and a brief run-through on Saturday.

We were guided backstage, kept from view while a jug-
gler performed, followed by a man with trained hairless

dogs. Then we were announced. Chairs were positioned. Charlie sat in the middle, the foot-high shoe lift and brace he wore visible before him.

We started with "Over the Waves." Dad played, as he usually did, with his eyes closed. My playing was incredibly clumsy, and the mikes amplified the mistakes. Fortunately, Charlie played a complex guitar. "There's a Tavern in the Town" was our next number, followed by "Red Wing." Charlie was halfway through his song when a wag started flinging pennies — a few at first, then a flurry. Some struck our faces. They spun like small saucers, stinging where they struck. Someone shouted "Crip!" at Charlie. Dad halted the performance, and we left the stage. The announcer expressed dismay and asked for a big round of applause. We'd been mocked for our poverty, I was sure! We should have worn cowboy clothes. Dad believed that another band we'd beaten out for the engagement was responsible. Charlie laughed, saying he wasn't in good voice anyhow.

On the way home, Dad told me not to be discouraged — I had played well. He asked me to join the band when dance-hall dates arose. He said they needed me.

Human and Animal

With their usual reticence about personal matters, particularly sexual ones, my parents obscured the fact of my brother's condition: His foreskin was nonretractable and required an operation. My own ignorance of such matters smacked of an embarrassing naïveté. Not until I learned about sex from the Jollys was I aware that you could retract your foreskin without harming your penis, like peeling back your eyelids. Nor had I thought much about circumcision — I had read the word in the Bible, but I had no real idea of its meaning. I interpreted the ancient Hebrews' propensity for chopping off their foreskins as yet another instance of tribal mayhem, a violation of God's creation: If He had not meant for men to have foreskins, He would not have made them.

When Everett returned home from Dr. Oldfield's office, he was in pain, and when he took off his pants to go to bed, I saw the bandage. My dad, in a matter-of-fact tone, embroidered the truth: "The doctor," he said, "cut off the end of his peter." My brother was probably the first member of my family to be clipped since progenitor Tunis Peters came to America in the eighteenth century.

Two days later, my uncle appeared with a set of knives, ready to castrate our bull, dropped by Lady the previous summer. Gelded, he would be gentle, increase his weight fast, and produce sweeter meat. I was to hold the ropes that secured him to his stall.

Dad and my uncle wrestled the bull to the floor, roping him. "Hold on hard," my uncle said. He knelt near the exposed belly, held up a knife, tested its sharpness with his thumb, and then brought it swiftly down and slit the bull's scrotum. As the bull bellowed and writhed, my uncle loosened the large, bean-shaped gonads and flung them into the chicken yard for the hens to eat. He poured turpentine and oil over the incision. Once untied, the bull rose and stood near the barn with his legs spread. "Fetch him some water, Bob," said my uncle.

Preparations for Winter

We inspected the house for deterioration, scraped off old plaster, and rechinked the logs with moss, which we secured by nailing small pincherry branches over it and smeared the whole with plaster. The roof required new tar paper. We rechinked the windows. Since we lacked storm sashes, the heat loss was enormous. On those parts of the house not built of logs, we nailed shiplap over defective boards. We cleared the cellar of debris and took out the old sand in buckets, replacing it with fresh sand for burying carrots, turnips, and potatoes. Finally, we banked an earth and straw mixture all around, covering a foot or so of the outside walls. This would prevent cold drafts from coming in under the floorboards.

After winterizing the house, we proceeded with the farm buildings and the outhouse. There was not much one could do to insulate the latter. Tar paper gave some protection, but on many mornings, after a blizzard had swept the seats with snow, you cleaned the seat with your glove, dropped your trousers, and planted your hams on the icy boards. We never used chamber pots unless we were ill. The smaller children, afraid of the dark, had to be accompanied to the outhouse by parents or older children holding flashlights.

By autumn we had cut the winter's hay. Much of it Dad mowed with a scythe, sweeping practiced swathes through stands of timothy and clover. He cut marsh grass also, mixed with domestic grass. Marsh grass blades were like razors. Cattle loved their seeded heads. Dad also bought two tons of alfalfa from Kula, who always had a surplus. And my uncle gave us hay for helping him harvest his. I loved riding on the horse-drawn wagon, stacking hay as it was pitched up. We fashioned large mounds near the barn, covering it with tarps. Stacked properly, these formed their own watershed, the rain seldom permeating more than an inch or two. For bedding we bought oat straw from Kula.

The most demanding autumn chore was gathering firewood. After the first heavy snow, in early November, the woods would be impassable.

Starting in midsummer we spent hours in our woodlands cutting, trimming, and piling poplar, birch, and pitch pine. The largest trees were about six inches in diameter. Most were smaller. Poplars, the softest of the woods, grew almost as fast as grass. White birch were slower, and oaks and maples slower still. A mix of birch, poplar, and pine produced the hottest fires.

We piled trimmed branches to dry for spring burning. We dragged the trees to the road and loaded them on a stoneboat; then, using my uncle's horses, we drew the wood home. Each year Dad sawed some forty cords. We were piling the last chunks into ricks during the first snowstorm.

Dad built our saw rig from a Model T engine with a large circular saw blade. The engine had to be throttled. A movable six-foot rack attached to the motor by leather strips fed logs to the saw. By pressing his thigh against the rack and guiding the log, Dad worked efficiently, estimating lengths suitable for the fireboxes. When released, the rack fell back, caught by the thongs. Some of the sawdust we sprinkled over the henhouse floor. The rest we used for burying ice. In the spring, the sawdust mulched the garden.

My sister and I piled the wood into ricks. I split the larger chunks, cross-piling them as rick ends. The object was to keep the rick as even as possible. If chunks held stubborn knots, you tried to find a place for the knot to fit snugly so as not to weaken the wood piled above it. The first ricks we stored under a quasi-shed, a corrugated tin roof mounted on poplar logs embedded in the ground. At least some of the wood would stay dry. We sorted pieces, reserving the largest blocks for the living room heater.

Dance Hall

At least twice a month we played music at Sam's Tavern, a roadhouse on the outskirts of Eagle River. Yet another of the low-timbered structures indigenous to the area, Sam's flourished outside the city limits, immune to raids from law enforcement officers. During Prohibition, the owner, Sam Capich, carried on a lucrative bootleg business there, or so it was rumored.

Capich was a short, rotund Czech in his late thirties who wore his black hair slicked. Generous-minded patrons said he deserved to be rich because he had an insane wife living at the back of the tavern. Occasionally we heard her screaming. Barring illness, Capich was behind his bar from 10 A.M. until 2:30 or 3:00 A.M. He seldom said much, smoked endless cigars, and showed his fondness for my dad by sending him rounds of beer between musical sets.

When we arrived at 9 P.M., a few patrons were gathered near the dance floor, waiting. Dad and Charlie had a beer at the bar, while I drank soda pop. We were scheduled to play until 1 A.M. Of the $30 we received as wages, Dad gave me $7. We wore slacks and plaid wool shirts. Our tunes, played on fiddle, accordion, mandolin, and guitar, were always the same—folk songs and popular songs from Dad's youth. He'd say that people liked the "old" music best. When we were ready to perform, Capich disconnected the loudspeakers, limiting the jukebox music to the bar area. The hall, paneled with knotty pine, was oblong, with an upright piano at the far end.

By 10:00 the floor was crowded. Among the regulars were Vic Barnes and his wife, Rosie. They were in their late twenties and poor. Rosie was slender, tall, somewhat horse-faced, with masses of brunette curls piled on her head, set off with flapper bangs. She wore much makeup. By 11:00 Vic was dead drunk. Rosie then had a good time, mainly with Ira Castleton, a fiftyish bachelor with a reputation as a lecher, who rarely missed a dance. Occasionally, Rosie would disappear from Castleton and trip out to the cars with another man. When Castleton found her, he would drag her off to his place, leaving Vic to fend for himself. On one outrageous evening, an Indian "had" Rosie behind the piano. A cluster of people gathered to observe. I got a glimpse before Dad drew me away.

Playing at Sam's Tavern produced dilemmas in my life. First, there was my religiosity. I was superintendent of the

Lutheran Sunday school; prayed with fervent regularity and was thinking of the ministry as a career. Pitted against all this were my strong sexual impulses. My prudishness won out. I saw the town as a Sodom or Gomorrah, and I appointed myself guarantor of my mother's interests. Dad was not to flirt with other women, and he must not drink too much. When he seemed about to hoist the telling glass of whiskey or beer, I nagged him. He was patient, and I don't recall his ever being drunk.

My own libido, on its silver chain, threatened to break loose as some handsome youth or maiden waltzed by. Was I doing the Devil's work? Whenever I expressed my doubts, Dad said we were not responsible — people chose their lives, and we had no business criticizing them. We were there to make the best music we could.

We played for Capich until I was a junior in high school, when he closed his dance hall, pleading poor receipts, too many fights, hassles from the sheriff, and his mad wife's cancer.

Fights

To stifle the numerous quarrels Margie and I had that summer, my mother would declare, "Just wait till you get to high school. Those guys are tough. They'll knock your block off."

My worst quarrel with Margie occurred a week before high school, the week after the county fair. To play pig family we formed a circle of kitchen chairs on the grass. Our conflict was over which of us would play the sow. Margie felt that a male should always play the boar, lingering at the back of the pen digging up roots while the lucky sow lay on her side squirting forth piglets. For a convincing porcine look, we wore Dad's heavy winter coats.

I would, for once, be the sow! I grabbed the coat my sister preferred, put it on, and flopped down in birth throes. I loved the delicious sensation of birthing. Squirt. Squirt. Squirt. When I turned to lick the piglets, Margie kicked at me and yelled. I fought back, spraining her hand. She announced she would drown herself in the lake.

I called her bluff, waved good-bye, and took the coats and chairs back into the house. Half an hour later, I began to worry, filling in time with some desultory hoeing in the flower garden. I started for the lake, near panic. No signs near shore of her shoes or clothes, no footprints, no evidence of a drowned person in the water. If she had indeed jumped, she had drifted into the cranberry marsh, out of sight.

I returned home. As I passed a hayrick, crying, Margie jumped out laughing. "Served you right," she said. I felt both angry and relieved.

From this point on, we played few childhood games. Within a few days her menstrual cycles began. Mom was in the Rhinelander Hospital having her goiter removed. Dad sent Margie to Aunt Kate to explain the facts of life and chose the occasion for my own sex education — or at least he tried. He explained "monthlies" and said it was time I "fucked" a girl. I should cross the road and take Celia Kula into the woods and "do it." I was shocked. The paradox of women as both citadels of purity — this is how I saw my mother, and was how my father conditioned me to see her — and licentious whores was painful.

In high school, since I was only twelve, I needed to employ my wits in complex ways. Whenever older boys threatened, I diverted hostility through a trick Osmo Makinnen taught me: Play subservient. Flatter your threatener by asking for information; for instance, what wrench does he use for loosening the lug nuts on his car? What is the largest pike he's ever hooked? What gym shoes are best? The questions were legion; the skill came in thinking of them fast enough to deflect hostilities. Even if a gang

threatened, the ploy worked: Regale the leader with a
question. I never once had to defend myself physically
throughout four years of high school.

Halloween

Possibilities for Halloween were always limited, and trick or
treat was not then the national ritual it has become. There
were very few other neighborhood families to plague.
Older boys attended dances in town. There wasn't even a
good graveyard nearby to liven things up.

The Jollys and I started the evening playing pinochle
rummy. We ate popcorn and raisin-filled cookies. At 9:00
we went to Hiram Ewald's. He was twenty and had quit high
school, preferring to stay home, as an only son, to work the
family farm. They sold milk. His dad told us to be careful;
if we got our butts shot full of rock salt, he wouldn't pick it
out.

We decided on two pranks—to tip over the outhouses at
the school and to fling rocks at Jorgensen, the Danish
bachelor. He lived alone, a victim, so it was said, of mustard
gas in the trenches.

Our first action was safe, since the school was closed and
there was no caretaker. The second was not so safe, since
Jorgensen had a reputation for waiting with a shotgun.

We tipped the outhouses, smeared the school windows
with soap, and then focused on Jorgensen. For our protection, we piled some scrap lumber over a small pit. If he
blasted away, we could scurry there and hide. George, we
decided, would attract Jorgensen's attention while we circled around in back and stoned his house. A dark moon
made our progress easier. We crept near, shouting a medley
of coyote calls, obscenities, and owl hoots and then hurling
a shower of stones. Suddenly, the front door burst open,
and Jorgensen emerged. There was an explosive flash.

As we scurried to our shelter, Jorgensen fired twice more and then returned to his house. The Jollys were for persisting in tipping over his outhouse. Since we'd approach from the rear, he wouldn't see us until he was too late. Hiram and I were for letting well enough alone. The old guy obviously meant business.

We settled into our bunker, cramped together. Hiram had a cigarette. We talked dirty. Hiram suggested we feel one another's erections, inside our pants. His felt like a milk bottle. We worked our way out of the bunker and stood listening; then we let out a few whoops in Jorgensen's direction and headed on up the road.

Gym

I dreaded gym class, so I delayed the perfunctory physical examination for weeks, hoping I would contract a disease rare enough to excuse me from class. Not only was I inexperienced at games, but I dreaded showing myself nude to strangers. The ball we had played at the Sundsteen elementary school was for kids. Even then, I could rarely catch a ball, and my balance was terrible — I had never ridden a bicycle. The only thing I did well was sprint over the rough terrain of those gravel country roads.

The principal, Mr. Kracht, known for his violent temper as "The Bull of the Woods," demanded to know why I was not attending gym. He was unimpressed when I said I lacked money for clothes. His ultimatum: "Attend on Monday! I will personally see you do!"

While the other students suited up, I stalled, removing my shirt as carefully as if it were glued to burn scabs. The locker door hid my lower body from view, and I faced the wall, preferring to show the world my rear rather than my privates. Once in the gym, I stood about with my arms awkwardly folded, intimidated by the prowess and agility of the other boys, especially those from town. When it came time to choose up sides for games, I was always chosen last. I avoided showers until the gym teacher threatened to strip and scrub me himself. "We don't want you stinking in class," he said. Again, I lingered, disrobing slowly, waiting for the other boys to finish. Draping my towel in front of me, I'd make my way to the end shower, face the wall, and bathe. Weeks elapsed before I was able to linger and enjoy the hot spray, a treat indeed considering our primitive bathing conditions at home.

Eventually, one of the flashiest town boys, Augie La Renzie, took an interest in me. I helped him with Latin declensions. He was curly-haired, funny, incredibly agile, and popular with both girls and boys. In his freshman year he made varsity basketball. During free periods, we would meet at the gym, where he gave me pointers on basketball. I was soon fairly adept at free throws. Augie also gave me health advice: Never wear someone else's jock strap; keep the venison out of your teeth; stop using brilliantine. He grew up to marry the county judge's daughter and became a World War II ace and a commercial pilot.

Esther Austin

The subject I did poorest in, math, was taught by my favorite teacher, Esther Austin. She was a short brunette in her thirties, unmarried, the daughter of the county superintendent of schools. Her standards for thoroughness and neatness were high, and she sought out students for special attention, especially those with adjustment problems. I was one of her favorites, although I did not know it then. My almost pathological shyness struck her — she was working on a masters degree in psychology at the University of Wisconsin. After algebra one day, she asked me if I would like to compete for the regional oratory competition. I harbored fantasies of being a lawyer or a teacher and knew that speaking skills mattered. And, Miss Crocker, the grade school teacher, had said I had a gift for public speaking.

Three times a week, during lunch hour, I would sit in Miss Austin's classroom rehearsing my oration, "Europe and the Jews," procured from a forensics bureau. Miss Austin mouthed the phrases while I recited them. She struggled to convince me that oratory does not mean shouting.

I brought Miss Austin flowers and fruit. I told her secrets I wouldn't have told my own mother. Years later, I discovered she had kept an ongoing "behavior journal," actually awarding points for my victories over shyness. She had set up special opportunities in class for me to gain self-confidence and she gave positive marks for those weeks when I confided in her less than I had earlier — evidence that I was maturing. She recorded whatever I told her of my feelings, my family, and other students. She encouraged me to think of girls. We had three-person committees who occasionally conducted class, having worked out in advance some difficult algebraic problem. She always appointed me to serve with girls.

One summer I worked for her father installing new insulation in the Austin attic. Mr. Austin got me a job cutting lawns and trimming bushes at the Ellis mansion, a huge lumber baron's home being converted into a hospital. Once I had graduated and was in Madison at the university, I realized the extent of Miss Austin's devotion. She hired me to type her master's thesis. When the draft arrived, I was stunned to see that I was one of three former students observed and analyzed in her meticulous journals. Her behavioral study was greatly influenced by the progressive ideas of John Dewey and Alexander Meiklejohn. Setups of the sort she designed for us in her classes could be used to modify behavior and plot maturity.

Years later, whenever I visited Eagle River, I saw her. She never married, and she kept her body vigorous by daily summer swims in Eagle Lake. In her seventies, she fell senile. The last time I saw her, she did not know me. She remained in a time warp of reveries supervising interminable high school cafeteria lunchroom hours. When she was found wandering a few blocks from her home, thoroughly lost, the court appointed her friend the Congregational minister as her guardian. He sent her to a nursing home, where she lived for ten years before dying.

Culture

Dorothy Canfield stood for culture; Myron Goldgruber did not. Canfield taught Latin and English literature, was a former actress, resembled Marlene Dietrich, and loved emoting. She took all the parts of *Romeo and Juliet* during two weeks of classes. To most of us, her hamming was sheer artistry. She painted her face in a florid manner to emphasize her high cheekbones and smeared kohl around her eyes. She wore enormous topaz bracelets, rings, and a scimitar of brass around her neck. She wore gypsy blouses, usually white trimmed in delicate flowers, and colorful wool skirts bought from Indians on a trip through the Southwest. Only six students took her Latin I, which was more of a club than a class.

Goldgruber, the manual arts instructor, was a bitter contrast. One chose either his biology or his woodworking classes. I chose the latter, thinking that my farm experience would help and that I might acquire more useful skills. Moreover, I feared science.

I was a disaster. Goldgruber ridiculed my birdhouse built of birch branches, on which I had spent hours trimming, tacking with finishing nails, cutting an entry hole, and even drawing a window on colored paper. He held the flimsy creation up before the class and said, "A girl must have made this." His voice was latent with rage. He held it between his palms and crushed it. "Now, Robert," he declared, dumping the mess on my desk, "have your mother build you a real birdhouse! No bird would live in this one!" Flushed with disgrace, I never returned to his class. I tried to soothe myself by saying that birdhouses have nothing to do with art. I would be an artist! My hunger was enormous. Ignorance floated in my mind like so much jetsam.

My awareness of classical music came unexpectedly. Another freshman, John Roesch, whose family were aristocratic Germans and whose father lost a lucrative business in Chicago during the 1920s, lived on Cranberry Lake. He seemed to have read everything; and he recited Shelley and Keats. His primary enthusiasm was for Richard Wagner. His mother was a professional musician, and he had trained for tenor roles. He loaned me an album, "Great Moments from the Ring Cycle," which I kept for a month, playing it daily on our wind-up Victrola. The album included synopses of the operas, the text of the arias, and notes on the singers. I loved "The Ride of the Valkyries."

Typewriter

High school intensified my desire to write, but I had no idea what, when, or how. Shortly, I busied myself writing a "novel" on the plight of the Czech town of Lidice. The Germans had taken the entire town hostage, killing everyone.

My image of myself was romantic. Not only should I fashion beautiful word patterns, but the physical properties of my book must be beautiful. I wrote "Lidice" in an old wallpaper book given to me by the owner of the hardware store. Each page, according to my fantasy, would be beautiful. It didn't matter that reading would be difficult, depending on the intricacies of the wallpaper designs. My

opening pages screamed drama as the Germans calmly
lined up all the women and children for slaughter. They
wanted the men to witness the carnage before they died. I
focused on a young mother with babe in arms, a figure
calculated to engender pity and terror in my readers. Like
many of my projects, this one never came to fruition. How
to sustain and complete a novel? Was it a matter of inspiration? Or of diligence and labor? Again, my romantic
notions placed inspiration far ahead of sweat, and once the
inspiration ebbed I was unable to go on, although "Lidice"
reached some fifty wallpaper-book pages.

I believed that if I had a typewriter, I would write more,
and better. The Sears catalogue featured a rebuilt Underwood for $30, complete with typing manual. I saved money,
primarily from playing guitar with Dad at dances, and sent
for one.

When the Underwood arrived, my enthusiasm outran
my diligence. I meant to start typing as soon as I had
unwrapped the machine, but I felt stymied. I detested the
time-consuming and boring drills outlined in the manual. I
did start to peck away at fundamentals, though it was not
until I took typing at school that I developed speed and
accuracy. I discovered, too, what I should have known all
along: The Underwood made no difference to my writing;
there were no shortcuts. I never typed any of "Lidice."

Fortunately, the typewriter was durable, unlike the tiny
movie projector I had earned as a premium for selling salve
the preceding spring. The premium catalogue had promised great fun with this "indestructible" projector, touting it
as "much more than a toy." To get it I had sold twenty boxes
of salve. Since we had no electricity, it would run on kerosene. Filmstrips were included.

The machine resembled a small smudge stove, with a pot
for burning kerosene, a short tube fitted with a lens, and a
crank and sprockets. There was a single filmstrip, of Betty
Boop, a sequence of ten frames. Making one's own trans-
parencies for casting on the wall supposedly was easy. With

much anticipation we tacked up a bed sheet, arranged chairs in a row, and made up fake tickets. Alas, I couldn't make the smudge pot work. Finally, when the smoke cleared, I managed to cast a faint image of Betty on the sheet. The machine was a fraud.

Something eluded me, something a youth with a practical turn of mind might understand. Near tears, I returned the machine to its box and never looked at it again. To this day, I approach most gadgets with trepidation. As for the typewriter, I finally became a proficient typist. During World War II this skill kept me from fighting as an inept rifleman on the German front.

Crappies and Bicycles

Less than a month before the lakes froze Dad bought a used rowboat. We tacked pieces of tin over the bottom, sealed them with tar, and then painted the boat. We would fish for crappies, a delicious new species planted in Minnow Lake by the State Fisheries Division.

The boat moved well, although there were still small leaks. We used cane poles. Crappies are fighters and, once hooked, tear off with the line. In half an hour we managed to land a dozen fish. We fried them in cornmeal dipped in egg batter. I mastered flensing so that the slabs were boneless.

The boat was a sign of our improving fortunes. Perhaps a bike would come next, although I had long since given up on ever owning one. Whenever I'd ask, my parents would say they didn't have the money and that you couldn't ride a bike in snow anyhow. Eventually, I accepted what seemed a fact of life in the country: Only town kids with sidewalks and paved streets had bikes.

In some ways I was glad, since all machines confounded me. I could never generate much interest in our family car, despite Dad's hopes. He kept saying that machines were "simple." I would wait nearby while he worked under his Ford, the lower half of his body protruding like the legs of a huge frog. When I helped him clean valves or adjust brakes, the intervals of waiting seemed interminable. Cleaning valves with steel wool was not my idea of fun. To Dad the intricacies of engines had beauty and grace. He would tell my mother in great detail what exactly he had done to regenerate a motor or to find the cause of a mechanical failure.

If I couldn't have a bicycle, I hoped we'd buy an Aladdin mantle lamp, to facilitate reading. The Botterons used one, and they weren't much better off than we were. The little mesh bags attached inside the globe held a mixture of air and kerosene that produced a wonderfully white light. Our single-wick lamps, even when the globes had been freshly cleaned with crumpled newspaper, cast such a weak orange-tinted glow that one's eyes tired easily, especially if the book had small print. When three of us were sitting at the table with schoolwork, we had arguments over where the lamp should stand. To avoid disputes, we measured the table, found the exact center, drew a circle, and agreed that there the lamp would remain. Those who couldn't see would have to hunch over so that they could. On winter evenings we vied for the favored spot nearest the heating stove. If you lost, you sat across the table with a blanket draped over your shoulders. The Aladdin lamp, with its white glass shade hand-painted with roses, when it came, shed a lovely light.

First Snowstorm

The glorious close of October, a halcyon stretch of Indian summer, faded as brilliantly hued maple leaves turned from reds to livid purples and browns, from yellows to dull ambers, and fell from the trees, leaving the branches bare. Poplar, aspen, birch, pincherry, and oak leaves, though not as colorful, paled and drifted as mulch to the ground. Intermittent chilling rains soaked those leaves still on the trees, hastening their demise. Flights of honking geese in elaborate formations flew south, following air currents so far above the earth the birds were almost invisible. Skunks and weasels nervously explored the henhouse for possible entries, hunting for fat meals against a possibly barren winter. Chickadees appeared, skittering for seeds on dried goldenrods, asters, and jimsonweed. Raucous crows pecked the last seeds from rotting sunflower heads and from ergot-covered ears of corn remaining in the fields. Blue jays screamed from the trees, where they had drilled holes and stuffed them with acorns. Our hens had grown thick new feathers. Pullets laid their first eggs. The dog's fur thickened. Lady continued to graze in the fields, but the grass had either turned brown or, though remaining green, had stopped growing. In the evenings, fogs rolled in from the swamps, depositing hoar frosts. Rain pools and groundwater near the pump were glassed with thin ice. Each day the air was chilled with mists. Indoors, we lit early-morning fires, banking them throughout the day. Even then, water left overnight in the kitchen in the pan we used for washing our hands and faces froze. We wore mackinaw jackets when we did chores and exchanged summer underwear for long johns. The first snowstorm materialized late one afternoon. The morning had been sunny with a brisk northerly breeze. Skies were clear. Shortly before 4 P.M., fast-moving dark clouds laden with moisture drifted in, shrouding the earth. The air suddenly smelled metallic, a fusion of brass and zinc absorbed from the huge clouds. At the sign of the first flakes, we put on our coats and went outside. We held our arms out and turned in slow circles, our faces thrown back, our mouths open, drinking in the huge flakes. Within minutes, the snow was so dense we were unable to see the barn. Woodpiles were capped with snow.

Light drifts formed near the road and swirled around the corner of the house, leaving bare patches where current vectors were strong.

When Margie, Nell, and Everett returned to the house, I stayed outside, luxuriating in the snow. The powdery drifts were now large enough to tumble about in, which I did, starting near the house and ending up at the bottom of the small hill leading to the strawberry patch. I lay spread-eagled, loving the feel of the flakes on my skin. I removed my gloves and thrust my fingers deep in the snow. I rolled over on my stomach, as if the white ground were a lover. Smother me, winter! Smother me! Nature's cyclical roll was intact, moving to its next stage, whirling man, animal, plant, and tree along its course. Next year at this time I would have changed, as my life gyrated, impelling me through my seasons, my final winter a gentle chilly breath present in all of the others. My cycle was unique; there could be no other one quite like it.